Museum of Art, Carnegie Institute
Collection Handbook

Andy Warhol (American, b. 1928), *Andrew Carnegie*, 1981
acrylic and silkscreen on canvas, 98 x 79 in. (248.9 x 200.7 cm.)
Richard M. Scaife American Paintings Fund, 81.107

Carnegie Institute and Carnegie Library of Pittsburgh in the 1940s.

A view in 1985 of Sarah Scaife Gallery addition to Carnegie Institute.

the preferences of the Museum of Art's directors and trustees, in the decades following Andrew Carnegie's death the Carnegie International became more obviously conservative as modernism advanced its position as the significant artistic direction of the twentieth century. Relatively little avant-garde art was included in the exhibitions, and it was not until 1927, when Matisse won the Carnegie Prize, that a modernist was accorded high recognition. Although Bonnard and Matisse did sit on the International juries of award in the 1920s, they were the exceptions, and neither of these great painters' work was purchased for the collection until the 1960s. The first really important twentieth-century European modernist painting to enter the collection was Rouault's *The Old King*, which was purchased in 1940 amid great controversy. In fact, for the first half-century of the museum's development, virtually all additions to the collection were superior examples of academic or representational American and European painting.

In the 1950s, the leadership of director Gordon Bailey Washburn and the encouragement of Pittsburgh collector G. David Thompson revitalized the museum, and the Carnegie International exhibitions re-emerged in the post-war era as important and influential shows of the new avant-garde style of Abstract Expressionism. The special international flavor of Carnegie Institute's collection is very much a result of the acquisitions of the period, when important American Abstract Expressionist paintings such as de Kooning's *Woman VI* and Kline's *Siegfried* were purchased from International exhibitions along with many canvases by the leading European artists working in Abstract Expressionist styles. Receptivity to European and American contemporary avant-garde art is one of Washburn's and Thompson's legacies to Pittsburgh.

While the 1950s are distinguished for additions of contemporary art to the permanent collection, the sixties and seventies are remarkable for the significant growth of part of the historical collection. Art patron Sarah Mellon Scaife determined to create for Pittsburgh an important assemblage of paintings. With her commitment and the discerning guidance of director Leon A. Arkus, the Museum of Art thus embarked on its first major collecting campaign. The result of Mrs. Scaife's generosity, and that of her family after her death in 1965, is a group of remarkably fine pictures, primarily Impressionist and Post-Impressionist works, that includes such masterpieces as Monet's *Water Lilies,* Bonnard's *Nude in Bathtub,* and Matisse's *The Thousand and One Nights.*

Most other additions to the historical collection during the last two decades have been examples of late nineteenth- and early twentieth-century American art. The museum has purchased these to represent aspects of the American artistic endeavor that were not in the Internationals but are now recognized as significant; for instance, Luminism, still-life painting, and the abstract art of the 1930s. The American collection has greatly benefited from the commitment of Edith H. Fisher, who has made possible a number of the museum's important recent purchases and has built, in consultation with the museum, a private collection of early twentieth-century modernist art that is an intended gift to Carnegie Institute and fills significant absences in the collection.

In 1980 The A. W. Mellon Educational and Charitable Trust made a large grant endowing the perpetuation of the Carnegie International. This grant coincided with a new enthusiasm for great international exhibitions after several decades in which the art world had questioned their value. The Museum of Art has recognized that, with its unique tradition of the Carnegie International, it has good reason, and perhaps historical imperative, to concentrate on acquiring contemporary works, especially those exhibited in the Internationals. No other American museum owes as much to the symbiotic relationship that can exist between its special exhibitions program and the development of its permanent collection, and it is a testament to Andrew Carnegie's perspicacity that he recognized this potential from the beginning.

grants from Mrs. John Berdan and the Richard King Mellon Foundation. Purchases were made as well in the areas of Egyptian and classical antiquities, and, with Walter Reed Hovey's gift in 1973 of his collection of Oriental ceramics, the museum's Asiatic holdings took on much greater significance. More recent gifts by James B. Austin from his important collection of Japanese prints have further enhanced the expanding Oriental collection.

In the 1980s the decorative arts collections policy has had a somewhat closer focus than in earlier years. Although the ancient and Oriental collections remain important to the scope of the museum, and gifts are warmly encouraged, most curatorial attention has been directed toward developing the areas of greatest strength, European and American (including Western Pennsylvania) decorative arts. The eighteenth-century holdings continue to be enhanced, and the museum is energetically acquiring decorative arts objects that will complement eras already well represented in the paintings collection, namely 1850 to the present. The intention is to acquire masterworks rather than to assemble a comprehensive historical collection. The benefit of this policy became especially clear in the 1984 reinstallation of the Scaife Galleries when important works from the decorative arts collection joined the paintings and sculpture already on display there. The reinstallation, honoring the tenth anniversary of the Sarah Scaife Gallery, was based on the concept that the integration in a chronological sequence of the decorative and the fine arts creates a richer cultural and artistic context.

The Museum of Art has enjoyed rapid growth in its collection, facilities, program, and staff in the last twenty-five years; but it is important to note that before this time almost all the museum's resources were committed to the organization of the Carnegie International and that the museum did not give the same emphasis to the development, preservation, study, and interpretation of its collection that most major museums had long since initiated. While its history might, on the one hand, be regarded as somewhat dilatory, the museum possesses, on the other hand, both a fascinating tradition and a youthful vitality unusual in a mature institution serving a city as established as Pittsburgh. This particular history underscores the importance of the museums's now vigorous commitment to collection development.

Sarcophagus c. 225 A.D.

marble, 18 ¼ x 71 ¼ x 22 ¼ in. (43.8 x 181 x 56.5 cm.)
Gift of Baroness Cassel van Doorn, 53.4.2

Chinese, Yuan Dynasty, 13th century

How awe-inspiring it must have been to the fourteenth-century pilgrim. This more than four-foot-tall head is all that remains of a magnificent sculpture of Kuan-yin. In its original setting in a temple in northern China, this piece would have been one of a group of carved Buddhas and bodhisattvas, all covered with bright pigments. The walls of the temple would also have been decorated with gorgeous frescoes of Buddhist scenes.

The colors of the paint would still have been quite fresh, for they had probably been applied a century before, when a resurgence of Buddhism followed the establishment of the Yuan Dynasty in 1279. Great numbers of sculptures and paintings were commissioned for the new and restored temples.

Kuan-yin was a central deity in the pantheon of the Mahayana schools of Buddhism then prevalent. The basic goal of its creed was enlightenment, which would assure release from the cycle of birth and rebirth and its inherent suffering. This release from the wheel of existence, called nirvana, was attainable by all sentient beings through good works and faith. Kuan-yin represents the ideal of the bodhisattva, a being (*sattva*) who has reached an enlightened state (*bodhi*) but foregoes final entry into nirvana to work for the salvation of all. As the manifestation of mercy and compassion, Kuan-yin became during this period the most widely revered bodhisattva throughout Asia, particularly in China and Japan.

The unknown master sculptor who created this head no doubt relied in part on earlier models or on copybooks with iconographic drawings. The hair, an elaborate chignon with two curls that descend from the temples, turn, and cross the ears, is in a style dating back to the T'ang Dynasty (618–906). The elongated earlobes are an iconographic feature common to images of both the Buddha and the bodhisattvas. It is thought to have originated with depictions of the Buddha after he renounced his royal heritage and left behind his worldly riches, including the ornate earrings whose weight had stretched his earlobes. Another of the traditional thirty-two signs of enlightenment is the urna, or luminous mark between the eyebrows. Here the jewel that was once placed in the forehead to represent the urna has been lost.

The divinity of the subject is communicated by the solemn, contemplative gaze of the downcast eyes. The elegant arches of the eyebrows accentuate the sense of aloofness in the expression. Yet the sculptor has also been able to transmit Kuan-yin's compassion in the modeling of the small, slightly sinuous mouth, with its hint of a smile. The deep, deceptively simple lines of the carving imbue the face with a dramatic presence and simultaneously transmit extraordinary grace and elegance. The loss over the centuries of the original polychrome, traces of which still remain, has actually served to enhance our appreciation of the consummate skill of the thirteenth-century artist who created this masterpiece.

FF

Head of Kuan-yin

wood with traces of paint, 52 in. (132.1 cm.)
Decorative Arts Purchase Fund and by exchange, 72.19

Indian, 13th century

Of the myriad works of art produced on the Indian subcontinent in over five thousand years, the bronzes of Tamilnadu are among the finest. Bronze casting in this area received a significant impetus around 1000 A.D., when the great king Rajaraja Chola ascended the throne in his capital city of Tanjore. The tradition grew strong enough to continue for several hundred years, but the most exquisite bronzes were produced during his reign. Their refined grace and impressive technique moved Auguste Rodin, in 1921, to collaborate on a book about them with A. K. Coomaraswamy, the premier historian of Indian art.

This image of the Hindu god Shiva stands on a double lotus base, supported by a square platform also inscribed with lotus petals. The finely finished figure wears only a short lower garment (*dhoti*) decorated with a floral design, its folds appearing to be symmetrical stripes. Around his waist is a jeweled belt. He is further adorned with bracelets, armlets, two necklaces, and a sinuous sacred thread draped from his left shoulder across his chest. His long hair, arranged in a *jata-bandha,* is held in place with an ornamental band. The precise, elaborate details, the fluttering ends of the garment and belt, the sharply defined facial features, and the fullness of the figure attest to its thirteenth-century date.

Sculpted and cast by anonymous artists, images like this one were created by men who from childhood learned their art from their fathers and the master artists of their bronze-working community. The works were commissioned by royalty and the wealthy as acts of religious devotion.

Shiva, one of the most important Hindu deities, has many manifestations. In this benign and gracious form, Shiva Vrisha-vahana (Shiva with his vehicle the bull), he was originally in the company of two other figures. His bull, Nandi, would have stood behind him, and his wife, the goddess Parvati, would have been on his right. His raised left elbow would have rested on the head of the bull, the gently curving fingers touching its forehead. A crooked stick (*vakra-danda-yudha*), made of either bronze or wood, would have been in his right hand. This particular Shiva image follows remarkably closely the descriptions given in Sanskrit iconographic texts, including the statements that he "should be standing with his right leg placed firmly on the ground and the left slightly bent . . ." and his left hand "should hang fully open so that the tip of the middle finger may reach the level of his own navel." Very few of these group images are preserved in their entirety.

Such bronzes were generally intended as processional images. They were not the objects of daily veneration in temple sanctuaries, but were housed in side chapels and carried out into the village or town on festival days. The holes in their bases allowed the images to be secured with ropes and bamboo poles. The iconographic group of Shiva Vrisha-vahana was carried, appropriately, on the back of a bull. The exceptional heaviness of these bronzes is a result of solid casting. The lost wax method was the prevalent technique, with surface finishing and polishing completed with fine tools.

ER

Large Head of Ichikawa Ebizō (Danjūrō V) c. 1796

woodblock, 12 ⅝ x 8 ⅜ in. (32.1 x 21.3 cm.)
Gift of James B. Austin, 85.23

Royal Brasscasters' Guild Workshop
Nigeria, Edo Kingdom of Benin

This "bronze" plaque represents a high-ranking chief in ceremonial war costume accompanied by a musician and arms bearer. The imagery is particularly appropriate to the time and circumstances of the plaque's creation. In the late sixteenth to early seventeenth centuries, the Edo Kingdom of Benin was at its height, encompassing much of what is today southern Nigeria. From its beginnings as a small city state, Benin emerged in the fifteenth century as a powerful warrior nation. When Portuguese explorers reached the area sometime between 1472 and 1486 they found a highly developed kingdom, engaged in territorial conquest, with whom they were able to establish diplomatic and trade relations. After the Portuguese came the Dutch, French, and English, and trade with these European nations became a mainstay of Benin imperial success.

This was also a period of artistic florescence in Benin. The guild of brasscasters (Igun Eronmwon), located in a special ward in the capital city, created magnificent copper alloy sculptures to glorify the king and court. These are called bronzes, even though their exact composition is not known, and some of them may actually be brass. Among them are over nine hundred decorative plaques that provide a testimony to court life at that time. A Dutch account from the first half of the seventeenth century describes, in the interior courtyards of the royal palace, "wooden pillars, from top to bottom covered with cast copper, on which are engraved the pictures of [Benin] war exploits and battles."

In this plaque a chief parades in ceremony with two attendants, whose diminished size is a reflection of their inferior social status. The chief is wearing a tall conical hat similar to one called *ogbovu* that high-ranking town chiefs in Benin wear today, made of a bark framework covered with red ceremonial cloth. The chief's thick choker of coral beads is likewise an indication of elevated title within the chiefly orders, and the ring of leopard claws around the chief's neck is a metonymic reference to the king of the forest animals, whose ferocity can drive away enemies. The bell below the leopard claws was worn by warriors to signal their positions in battle and to proclaim victory on their return home. The long garment is either made of or represents feathers, quite possibly those of the West African gray parrot, whose red tail feathers are considered effective in warding off evil. Along the hem of the garment are small calabashes of potions to strengthen warriors in battle. In his left hand the chief holds a leather shield, in his right a barbed spear.

A plaque of identical iconography in the Museum of Mankind, London, enables us to reconstruct the parts of this plaque that have been broken. We can assume that the figure on the chief's right was holding a leaf-shaped ceremonial sword called *eben* in his right hand; in his left he holds a sheaf of spears with a cap over the points. The other attendant is playing a side-blown trumpet and has the braided hairstyle common to musicians depicted in the plaques.

The upper corners of this plaque are broken, but its counterpart in the Museum of Mankind depicts a Portuguese head in each corner. Portuguese figures appear frequently in the iconography of this period as visual reminders of the wealth they brought to the Benin Kingdom at its period of greatest political and artistic achievement.

PB-A

Portable Altar

ivory, 8 ³⁄₈ x 6 ¹⁄₄ x 1 ¹⁄₈ in. (21.3 x 15.9 x 2.9 cm.)
Gift of Jeannine Byers, 56.3.1

Nicola di Maestro Antonio d'Ancona

Italian, Anconan, active 1472

This large and important early Renaissance altarpiece of the Madonna and Child with saints is the only signed and dated work by Nicola di Maestro Antonio d'Ancona, and in fact the only proof that he ever existed, as no documents relating to his life have yet been found. On the basis of this painting, Bernard Berenson in 1915 attributed seven other works to Nicola, and this total has since been expanded to seventeen.

Probably Carnegie Institute's painting once stood in the church of San Francesco della Scalla in Ancona, for the writer Alessandro Maggiore, in a guidebook of the town written in 1821, noted that this sanctuary housed an altarpiece painted in 1472, the date inscribed on the Pittsburgh painting. The altarpiece shows four saints adoring the Mother and Child, along with a diminutive female donor, whose small scale signifies her humility and her separation from the realm of the divine. The identity of the donor has not been established, but the saints are easily recognized by their attributes. On the far left stands Saint Leonard, the patron saint of prisoners, carrying his emblem, the leg shackle, and a book with raised gold ornament. Next to him is Saint Jerome, who can be identified by his book and by the lion with a wounded paw at his feet. To the right of the Madonna stands Saint John the Baptist, dressed in camel hair and holding a book and a staff with a cross attached to it. On the far right Saint Francis, dressed in the habit of the order he founded, stands in prayer, his hands bearing stigmata. (The town of Ancona was an important center of the Franciscan order, particularly of the Spiritualists, the more adamantly austere division of the sect.)

A fly, which casts a shadow, rests beside an apple on the platform of the Virgin's throne. These elements symbolize the evil that Christ overcame. The fly traditionally was associated with evil, pestilence, and Satan (in fact, one of the names for Satan, Beelzebub, means "Lord of the Flies"). The apple brings to mind the apple from the Tree of the Knowledge of Good and Evil that brought about man's fall (in Latin the word *malum* means both "apple" and "evil"). In contrast to these reminders of sinfulness and death, the red and white flowers in the nearby vase invoke Christ's mission on earth. Carnations traditionally were worn by brides, and in this context they serve to remind us of the symbolic marriage between Christ and His church. The white flowers symbolize the purity of Christ's birth, the red ones his sacrifice to save mankind.

The city of Ancona, on the eastern coast of Italy, was part of a region of Italy that absorbed the new artistic influences of the early Renaissance rather gradually. Consequently, the altarpiece contains a curious mixture of archaic and progressive elements. The figures are rendered with many strange linear distortions, such as the oversized thumbs of Saint Leonard and the bulging veins of Saint John the Baptist, which swirl in harmony with the floral motif on the gold background. Such features derive from the International Gothic style, as do the egg tempera medium and the gold background. On the other hand, the painting contains elements, like the classical motifs on the Virgin's throne, and the tile pavement and distant landscape which are drawn in accurate one-point perspective, that reflect the Renaissance rediscovery of classical antiquity and discovery of geometric perspective.

HA

Virgin Mary   c. 1430 – 50

limestone, 51 ¾ x 16 ½ x 12 ⅝ in. (131.4 x 41.9 x 32.1 cm.)
Gift of Baroness Cassel van Doorn, 58.25.30

Benedetto Buglioni

Italian, 1459/60 – 1520

Benedetto Buglioni, according to Giorgio Vasari's *Lives of the Painters, Sculptors and Architects,* illicitly obtained the secret of glazing terracotta from a woman of the house of Andrea Della Robbia, showing that industrial espionage was rife even in the fifteenth century. Vasari's gossipy insights into the artistic community in Florence show, along with the works themselves, that there was at least one well-established workshop besides the Della Robbia's that produced monumental, sculptural, tin-glazed earthenware in Florence between 1480 and 1520. This shop was headed by Benedetto Buglioni.

The technique of tin-glazing earthenware was well established in Italy by the fifteenth century. Its use, however, was confined to traditionally functional wares such as plates, medicine jars, and bowls until Luca Della Robbia (1399/1400–1482) began to substitute tin-glazed earthenware for marble to produce a wide variety of sculptural reliefs. Luca's workshop and the traditions he established were continued by his nephew Andrea Della Robbia (1435–1525), and the success and popularity of the Della Robbia workshop no doubt encouraged Benedetto to follow the same path.

Very little is known about Buglioni's life. He was born and died in Florence, the son of a stonecutter. He married Lisabetta Mori in 1489 and is listed in the marriage document as a sculptor, which indicates the status of his workshop. Several monuments can be ascribed to him, and the first fully documented work, *Christ in Hades,* dates from 1484. In 1504 Buglioni was chosen, with the best Florentine artists, to select the site for Michelangelo's *David,* which suggests his standing in the artistic community.

On the predella of the *Lamentation* are the heraldic devices of the Trotti and Davanzati families, who may have commissioned the work for a Franciscan church or monastery, a possibility suggested by the rather unusual iconographic placement of St. Francis of Assisi in the mourning group. This relief is not a free-standing sculpture but, like most of the pieces from the Della Robbia and Buglioni workshops, was intended for installation in an architectural setting.

For this type of relief sculpture glazed clay had certain advantages over marble: it was cheaper, easier to model, and, more importantly, could be brightly polychromed. Color plays an important part in Buglioni's work, especially in his later period. In the *Lamentation over the Dead Christ* the limp body of Christ is gently supported by the Virgin Mary with St. John to her right and St. Francis to her left. Their dark robes convey the somberness of the scene and emphasize the figures' white heads and hands as well as the white body of the dead man. The focal point is not only the dead Christ but also the emotion—serene, graceful, and self-contained—of St. John, St. Francis, and the Virgin. The viewer is not invited to share their sorrow; it is too personal. But the tranquil calm of the scene is disturbed by the presence of the cross. Although it is modeled in low relief, the bright yellow cross, with its strong lines, leaps from the background as a vivid reminder of the horrendous manner of Christ's death.

SN

Lamentation over the Dead Christ   c. 1520

tin-glazed earthenware, 52 x 31 x 7 ¼ in. (132.1 x 78.7 x 18.4 cm.)
Mr. and Mrs. George L. Craig, Jr., Fund, 68.30

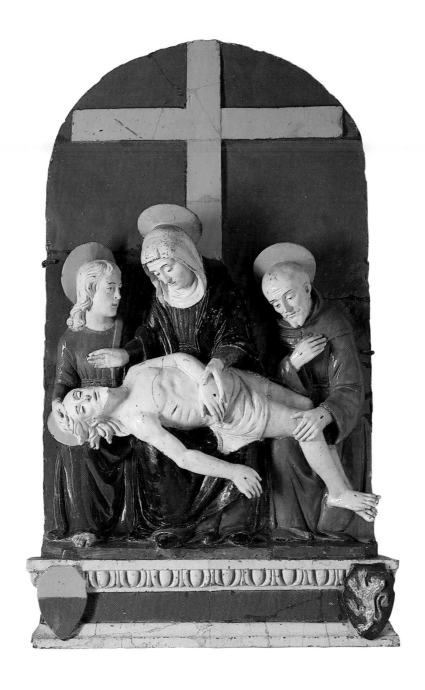

Pietro di Cristoforo Vannucci, called Il Perugino

Italian, Umbrian, c. 1450–1523

Pietro Vannucci, now generally known as Il Perugino after his adopted home of Perugia in the hills of Umbria, is best known today as Raphael's teacher. His paintings have a serene, pure quality, as in this example, with its calm figures placed against the clear and cloudless Umbrian sky, shaded to white at the horizon and set off with delicate trees.

Before 1796 the city of Perugia was wonderfully rich in the works of Perugino, but after Napoleon's conquest of Italy its art was plundered by the French. On March 27, 1797, six wagons drawn by twenty-four oxen bore away Perugia's finest treasures, and later Napoleon signed a decree to take away still more. This painting, which was first firmly documented in 1815 as the property of Napoleon's brother Lucien, probably left Perugia as part of this wartime loot.

The painting depicts St. Augustine, the Bishop of Hippo in North Africa, who is shown in Augustinian vestments with a bishop's crozier and mitre. In the background are four members of the Confraternity of St. Augustine. Confraternities were groups of lay individuals who banded together to do good works. They usually wore hoods over their faces so that their charitable acts would be known only to God. Probably this painting originally hung in a small chapel dedicated to the Confraternity of St. Augustine.

The style of the painting is characteristic of works executed by Perugino's studio in the years around 1500. Indeed, the face of St. Augustine is a stock face that occurs in a great many of Perugino's paintings, not only for other representations of this saint, but for priests, sages, and God the Father.

Three drawings related to the painting survive, the first in the Pierpont Morgan Library, New York; the second in the Clark Art Institute, Williamstown, Massachusetts; and the third in The Metropolitan Museum of Art, New York. According to Nicholas Turner, these drawings were all executed by the same hand but were not made by Perugino. All three drawings were traditionally attributed to Raphael before the turn of the century, when they were in the Constabile collection in Perugia, which raises the possibility that Raphael might have had a hand in the painting as well. More extensive study of Raphael's early work, however, will be required before it is possible either to confirm or reject this conjecture.

HA

Dish from Swan Service   1737 – 41

porcelain, 13 ¼ in. (33.7 cm.), diameter
Ailsa Mellon Bruce Collection, 70.32.1545

Johann Joachim Kändler
German, 1706 – 1775 (designer)

Meissen Factory
German, 1710 – present (maker)

The sculptural aesthetic played a crucial role in the early history of the Meissen factory. Skillful handling of three-dimensional form and design was the key to success, whether for a free-standing figure or a tureen with modeled handles and finial. The plasticity of functional though luxurious wares, such as tureens, was consistently significant and well handled at Meissen because sculpture was taken so seriously. The figure was a constant theme in the factory's production. But whereas the small, intimate, almost whimsical characters of the Commedia dell'Arte typify the Rococo aesthetic of the 1740s, figures with a piercing intensity, conceived on a grand scale in true Baroque taste, characterize the 1730s. *St. Paul,* from a set of the Twelve Apostles, is a culmination of this Baroque manner.

In the early 1720s Augustus the Strong, under the effects of *Porzellankrankheit* (porcelain disease), embarked on a project to fill his Japanese Palace, which already contained the largest collection of imported Oriental porcelain in the West, with Meissen porcelain. He ordered Meissen wares that imitated those from the East, but he also wanted his factory's works to surpass the Oriental examples. He proposed, among other seemingly impossible things, a series of monumental birds and animals and altarpieces with sacred sculpture, including life-size statues of the apostles. Although Augustus conceived of a sculptural force at Meissen, his ideas could not be realized until Johann Joachim Kändler joined the factory on June 22, 1731.

Kändler had been apprenticed to the court sculptor Benjamin Thomä. Augustus probably noticed the swift and skillful Kändler during one of his visits to Thomä's workshop and enticed him to Meissen. Although Kändler worked for the factory right up until his death in 1775, he continued to undertake monumental sculptural commissions, such as tombs, in wood and stone. That he never totally abandoned his original calling as a sculptor is clear from his work for Meissen. The death of Augustus the Strong in 1733 put an end to the more grandiose schemes for the Japanese Palace; but Meissen continued to produce large-scale figurative works, frequently commissioned by Augustus the Strong's son and successor, Augustus III, as political or personal gifts for influential individuals. As early as August 1735 Kändler was working on figures of St. Peter and St. Paul as part of a large altar garniture set for Cardinal Albani. The Albani *St. Paul* is about three centimeters smaller and of different design than the same figure in the slightly later sets of apostles.

Kändler's first set of apostles, with the newly modeled St. Peter and St. Paul, was produced in 1737–38, and by 1741 several sets had been made, some, like this *St. Paul,* with the Austrian Imperial coat-of-arms. The designs of these figures are so like those of the twelve huge marble apostles in St. John Lateran in Rome that they must derive from engravings or drawings of those monumental sculptures. The Lateran *St. Paul,* signed and dated 1708, and *St. Peter,* completed by 1713, were commissioned by Pope Clement XI, the uncle of Cardinal Albani, from Pierre-Etienne Monnot (1657–1733). Kändler's *St. Paul* is no mere pastiche, however, but a thoughtfully conceived figure with an aura of mystic intensity combined with worldly theatricality, inspired by the renowned Baroque sculptor Gian Lorenzo Bernini.

SN

Side Chair   c. 1740

walnut, walnut veneer, and needlework upholstery, 38 ⅜ x 21 ¼ x 17 ¾ in. (97.5 x 54 x 45.1 cm.)
Ailsa Mellon Bruce Fund, 83.38

Longton Hall

English, 1749–1760

English porcelain factories in the second half of the eighteenth century, unlike their European counterparts, did not receive royal patronage. They were forced to be economically viable from their very inception, in a period of great experiment, development, and change in the ceramic industry, stimulated by the industrial revolution. Many factories closed after only a few years, as backers withdrew their capital when favorable economic results failed to emerge. One such short-lived factory was Longton Hall, founded near Stoke-on-Trent, Staffordshire, in 1749 and dissolved in 1760.

Chelsea and Bow, the first factories to make porcelain on a commercial scale in England, did not go into production until around 1745, which meant Longton Hall entered the English porcelain arena in its early, formative stage. Because of this and its huge scale of production, the quality of wares made at Longton Hall was uneven, especially in the early years. In 1753 and again in 1755 the factory received fresh injections of capital and the quality of the clay body, glazes, potting, and modeling improved.

Cos-lettuce sauceboats were made from the first years of the factory's production. This pair, however, dates from about 1755, in the period of the factory's great technical advancement. They are crisply and delicately molded, as is evident in the superb arched stem handles and the applied buds at their base, and they represent the best wares produced by the factory.

The same high quality is seen in the painting of the red veins and green edges of the sauceboats' exterior leaves and their interior motifs. Polychrome decorating, less technical than modeling but equally important to the manufacturing process, also made great progress at the factory around 1755 because of two experienced and talented artists. In 1754 William Duesbury, an enameler, came from London to work at Longton Hall. He stayed only a couple of years before traveling a short distance east to become a partner in the Derby porcelain firm, but his presence continued to be felt at Longton Hall in the improved polychroming he inspired. In 1755 the artist John Hayfield, known for his paintings of continental views and classical ruins, joined the factory as a decorator. He was probably responsible for the detailed and exquisitely painted classical folly set in a hot, hilly landscape in the bottom of one of the sauceboats.

The early years of the English porcelain industry coincided with the establishment of the Rococo style in the country. Although porcelain did not play a leading role in the development of the style, it was admirably suited to it. Rococo taste delighted in the natural world. Botanical forms were not only painted onto the gleaming white porcelain but actually molded from it to provide the very structure of the object, taking naturalism to its zenith. The naturalistic form of these sauceboats, with the asymmetrical arrangement of the cos-lettuce leaves and the stem handles, captures the organic dynamism and frivolity of the exuberant Rococo style. The surface decorations on the interior of the sauceboats are also typical of the mid-eighteenth century. The botanical theme is continued in paint, and the floating insects near each lip, which derive from Oriental ceramics, are examples of *chinoiserie*, the adoption of Chinese decorative motifs in the West, an important element in Rococo design. Even the painted classical ruin, set mysteriously in a romantic landscape, is evocative of emotional Rococo taste rather than the formal, intellectual, Neo-Classicism that superseded it.

SN

Pair of Sauceboats   c. 1755

porcelain, 4 x 8 ⅛ x 4 ⅛ in. (10.2 x 20.6 x 10.5 cm.)
Ailsa Mellon Bruce Collection, 70.32.1914-15

Josiah Wedgwood and Thomas Bentley

English, active 1769–1780

The fine patina and play of light on the surface of this well-modeled bust of Sir Isaac Newton (1642–1727), signed by Wedgwood and Bentley, create the impression that it is made of bronze. The bust is, however, made of a clay body known as black basaltes.

Although black pottery had been made in the Staffordshire area of England by local potters since the early eighteenth century, it was not perfected until Josiah Wedgwood (1730–1795) actively tried to improve it around 1767. By late 1768 Wedgwood's experiments with a solid black body had progressed greatly, and in August of that year Wedgwood sent a pair of black vases, which he called "Etruscan," to an influential acquaintance, Miss Tarleton, the daughter of the Member of Parliament for Liverpool. In a letter he referred to these as an "offering of first fruits." The black body was extremely susceptible to changes in temperature during firing, and in the same letter Wedgwood noted that "every last vase in the kiln was destroyed." Gradually he minimized such problems and added the black body to his production line. By 1773 Wedgwood had renamed it black basaltes or black porcelaine, "Etruscan" being limited to black-bodied forms decorated with enamel or encaustic painting in the Greek Attic red-figure style.

In 1769 Wedgwood had gone into partnership with Thomas Bentley (1730–1780), a Liverpool merchant, and the basaltes body played an important role in establishing their early financial success. They officially opened their large factory near Stoke-on-Trent in June of 1769 and named it Etruria for the region in Italy inhabited by the Etruscans and for the arts of that classical civilization.

The partners' name for their factory reflected a new classical spirit that was perhaps the most important reason for the popularity and success of the black basaltes body. They were able to turn a growing interest in the arts of the Greek and Roman civilizations into a market for their basaltes because they produced objects, such as portrait busts, that were in concert with this new aesthetic. As they wrote in their 1779 catalogue: "The black Composition having the Appearance of *antique Bronze,* and so nearly agreeing in Properties with the Basaltes of the Aegyptians, no Substance can be better than this for Busts, Sphinxes, small Statues, &c. and it seems to us to be of great Consequence to preserve as many fine Works of Antiquity and of the present Age as we can, in this composition."

Wedgwood and Bentley were also hoping to appeal to the new intellectualism. They saw their basaltes busts as a stimulus to learning that would "most effectually prevent the Return of Ignorant and barbarous Ages." They therefore produced busts not only of famous Greeks and Romans but also of more modern "illustrious" men who embodied the Neo-Classical ideal of the Enlightenment, including poets, playwrights, and philosophers. They further encouraged comparison between the ancients and moderns by presenting their near contemporaries in a classical package. Although Newton was a seventeenth-century man, the modeling of his bust and its whole demeanor rely heavily on antique prototypes. The English philosopher, physicist, and mathematician from humble beginnings appears in the guise of a Roman dignitary.

SN

Fan Depicting Coronation of Louis XVI   c. 1775

silk, mother-of-pearl, gouache, gold and silver leaf, sequins, and silk and metallic thread,
10 ¼ x 19 ¼ x 1 ⅛ in. (26 x 48.9 x 2.9 cm.)
DuPuy Collection, D402

Probably Bohemian

This wine fountain, though English in style, is made from nonlead glass rather than the lead glass used in Anglo-Irish factories. Both the style and the material point to Bohemia as the fountain's country of origin.

Bohemia, now part of Czechoslovakia, has had a thriving glass industry since the fourteenth century. By the 1730s Bohemian nonlead glass products had found markets in about fifty major European cities, as well as in Baltimore, New York, and Mexico. At the end of the eighteenth century the most serious competition to Bohemian glass came from the English glass industry, which, dramatically improved by inventions such as Humphrey Perrott's furnace in 1734 and Josiah Wedgwood's pyrometer fifty years later, crested on the tide of the Industrial Revolution. In order to compete with the English, the Bohemians started to produce a line of wares that, like this wine fountain, were completely in keeping with English social customs and the Neo-Classical aesthetic that was popular in England in the last quarter of the eighteenth and the first few years of the nineteenth centuries.

The bowl of this fountain is urn-shaped, a ubiquitous Neo-Classical motif. Its spigoted form—rare in glass—is derived from more common examples in silver, such as tea and hot water urns. The brief popularity of the wine fountain form, and the fragility of glass as a material for such a utilitarian object, no doubt account for the rarity of this object, not to mention its missing glass tap.

At the time this fountain was created, fashion required glass to be thin, which made deep incisions impossible. Even the shallow cutting of the fountain's decoration, however, produced the desired effect of refracting light. The stylized leaf motif encircling the bowl, the flutes around the rim, and the facet-cut tapered panels around the base are all typical of late-eighteenth-century cut designs.

From about 1750 producers of elegant glassware faced stiff competition not only from each other, but from newly founded European porcelain factories. Porcelain won the contest at the tea table and for the dinner service itself, but glass triumphed when it came to wine and dessert wares. Handsome glass dessert and wine services, with up to five hundred matching pieces, glittered in the candlelight on fashionable turn-of-the-century dining tables. Wine services alone required not only a vast array of drinking vessels, but also decanters (up to twenty-four in a matching set), individual wine coolers with separate plates, finger bowls, and perhaps a wine fountain.

SN

Wine Fountain   c. 1790–1810

glass, 15 ¾ x 6 ⅝ in. (40 x 16.8 cm.)
Ailsa Mellon Bruce Fund, 83.58

William Blake
English, 1757–1827

William Blake, also a poet and religious mystic, ranks among the greatest English artists. He was an extraordinarily versatile painter, printmaker, and book illustrator, and his collections of poems, such as *Songs of Innocence* and *Songs of Experience,* identify him as the forerunner of the Romantics Wordsworth, Coleridge, Shelley, and Keats.

Blake was born the son of a hosier in London in 1757. He began his studies of art there at the age of ten and then apprenticed to the engraver James Basire, who acquainted him with Gothic design and the engravings of Old Masters such as Raphael, Michelangelo, and Dürer. In 1779, Blake briefly attended classes at the Royal Academy but was discouraged by what he perceived to be the desertion there of rigorous Neo-Classic academic principles.

From 1780 on, Blake exhibited at the Royal Academy and elsewhere but never earned a successful living. Before 1790 he concentrated on poetry, but later he began to illustrate his books, eloquently merging text and picture. Eventually Blake assigned greater importance to his illustrations, and by 1794–95 he began to issue them independently. Concurrently, he developed new reproduction processes, using a tacky pigment that imitated the effects of watercolor. Rendering themes from the Bible, Milton, and Shakespeare, Blake produced some of the most powerful, complex, and fantastical images in the history of art.

Blake's vision was so original and peculiar that it long denied him recognition and commercial success. Around the turn of the century, however, he finally acquired a patron, a minor civil servant named Thomas Butts. Butts commissioned illustrations of religious subjects, including *Faith, Hope, and Charity.*

In 1809, Blake held an exhibition of paintings at his brother's London house. It failed and he dropped from sight for almost a decade, though he continued to paint watercolors for Butts. Then in 1818 he met the landscape and portrait painter John Linnell, who became a constant patron, paying Blake for almost everything he painted and introducing him to a group of admirers, including Samuel Palmer and John Varley. Blake spent his last years on his monumental engraving projects *The Book of Job* and Dante's *Divine Comedy,* in which the artist reached new heights of symbolic and technical power.

Faith, Hope, and Charity is the best preserved of about fifty small tempera pictures on biblical themes that Butts commissioned in 1799. In mixing the pigments for these works, Blake claimed to have used a late Medieval recipe described by Cennini, but it may have been a mistake in translation that led him to use carpenter's glue as a binding medium rather than egg. It was the glue binder that produced the rich coloring of *Faith, Hope, and Charity,* but it also probably caused the unusual cracking and darkening of the picture surface.

Faith, Hope, and Charity illustrates I Corinthians 13:13: "And now abideth faith, hope, and charity, these three; but the greatest of these is charity." Blake depicted Faith deep in study and Hope as a prophetic recording angel. Charity stands benevolently over her seated companions, gently cradling two babies in her arms.

EAP

Lilies and Pelargoniums in a White Vase   1863

oil on canvas, 18 x 15 in. (45.7 x 38.1 cm.)
Museum purchase: bequest of Roy A. Hunt and gift of The Roy A. Hunt Foundation
in memory of Mr. and Mrs. Roy Arthur Hunt, 84.55

Camille Pissarro

French, 1830–1903

In the 1870s, when Pissarro painted this picture, Pontoise, stretching along the banks of the Oise twenty miles northwest of Paris, was a diversified country town that offered a wide range of subjects from the industrial to the idyllic. Factories dotted the riverside, new houses nudged up against thatched-roof cottages, and farmland surrounded the town as far as one could see. Pissarro made Pontoise his home for nearly twenty years, arriving with his family in 1866 and leaving in 1883. Although in the later 1860s he was forced to spend a lot of time in Paris selling his work, it is Pontoise that is most associated with Pissarro. During his years there, he developed his style in more than two hundred paintings that, as a group, placed him in the forefront of modernist art and put Pontoise on the artistic map.

This straightforward, warmly lit view of the entrance to the town was painted in the first year of Pissarro's return to Pontoise from a self-imposed exile in England during the Franco-Prussian war of 1870. Its unassuming subject matter is typical of the soft-spoken artist who in later years told his son Lucien, "Happy are those who see beauty in modest spots where others see nothing."

Like his seventeenth-century Dutch predecessors or the Barbizon artists of the mid-nineteenth century, Pissarro knew how to translate the quiet corners of his world into small poems. He provides easy access to this scene by stretching the road across the width of the canvas and having it rise up in a gentle curve. Its tans and greens can be read simultaneously as paint, light, and earth, an artful balance that Pissarro strikes throughout the picture. The road narrows quickly as it slopes past the large bushes and trees to the town beyond. The houses in the center receive the warmest yellow light, complementing the bright yellow-green foliage on the right. Pissarro's wonderful sense of color is also evident in the subtle browns of the houses on the left and the variety of contrasts on the right, particularly the green shutters in the house on the far right and the mauve material in the window.

The area surrounding this scene offered Pissarro more than he chose to paint, for this square, a link in a ring of public spaces that encircled the city, was generally a busy place. Moreover, had Pissarro turned around he could have painted a panoramic view of the Oise valley with several local monuments and the ramparts of the town at his feet. In opting for the simpler scene, Pissarro presents us with what has been called an anti-landscape, one that rejects the traditional elements of the picturesque, the romantic, the historic, and the monumental. Pissarro's scene, instead, is so close to everyday life that it could almost be considered mundane, a charge many contemporary critics leveled against Impressionist paintings. But Pissarro, like his Impressionist colleagues, sought to embody actual experience in his art and thus to express greater clarity and truth.

PT

The Great Bridge at Rouen   1896

oil on canvas, 29 ³⁄₁₆ x 36 ¼ in. (74.1 x 92.1 cm.)
Purchase, 00.9

Exhibited in the 1900 Carnegie International

Hilaire-Germain-Edgar Degas

French, 1834–1917

Preceded by at least four studies and related works, this loosely painted, compact scene is a striking example of what Degas meant when he said, "Painting a picture is like plotting a crime." Every element here is intricately related.

This is first apparent in the foreground, where Degas daringly locates the dingy white sheets of the bed. These are so thinly painted that they derive substance from the texture and color of the canvas. The various gray outlines suggest the contours of both the fabric and the bed, which extends beyond the frame on the right. These lines likewise create geometric patterns that echo in twisted ways those of the curtain above while countering the floral ones to the left.

Degas has radically divided the left half of the picture from the right with the glowing orange curtain that flows diagonally through the center of the scene and contrasts in both color and texture with the green tub and the decorative blue background. The division is further marked by the dark outlines of the bed. The more one looks at *The Bath,* the more it appears to be two pictures held together by irregular interlocked shapes— the strong echoes of the woman's form in the contours of the bed; the juxtaposition of critical parts like the head, arm, and tub with the curtain; the towel that parallels the curtain and merges with the sheets at the bottom of the canvas. It is difficult to tell how far the bath is from the bed or the wall, however, and it is hard to explain the dashes of paint below the tub, the woman's curiously defined head and shoulders, or the disappearance of her left arm.

These questions of form and the contrasts in the picture raise basic questions about painting itself. One such question, debated since the seventeenth century, which Degas may be reformulating here, pitted line against color—an argument that was continued into the nineteenth century by Ingres and Delacroix, two artists Degas admired and copied. This conflict may be felt in the drawing and the flat application of paint on the right as opposed to the play of color and the freer brushwork on the left. One can't help but feel, however, that Seurat's pointillism is also behind the large dots on the left.

Degas started painting women bathing or at their toilette around 1885. His subjects were prostitutes, the settings their bedrooms. Like many men of his time, Degas often went to brothels, though he saw them not just as pleasure spots but as meeting places, work settings, and arenas in which the complexities of modern urban life were played out. In this picture, the viewer has a proximity to the scene and a sense of connection to the woman. The connection is strained, however, by the unfinished qualities of the picture.

PT

The Bath   1890

oil on canvas, 31 ¹⁵/₁₆ x 45 ¾ in. (81.2 x 116.2 cm.)
Acquired through the generosity of Mrs. Alan M. Scaife, 62.37.1

Hilaire-Germain-Edgar Degas

French, 1834–1917

Born into a wealthy banking family, Edgar Degas maintained his upper-class attitudes and friends throughout his life despite the fact that he changed his name from the aristocratic de Gas in the 1860s, saw the family fortune depleted by bad investments in the following decade, and associated with the less well-bred Impressionists for more than forty years. Aloof, arrogant, and prejudiced, Degas was the modern Parisian par excellence.

At the same time, however, he was deeply interested in the drama of contemporary life in his rapidly expanding city of Paris. He wrote in his notebook that he wanted to "do a series" on the smoke of locomotives, chimneys, factories, and steamboats; on bakeries and bread; on night life and cafés. An habitué of the opera and ballet, the bordello, and the horse race, Degas relished the offerings of the capital and devoted much of his life to rendering them.

Degas was also a great portraitist, an indication of his commitment to realism and his interest in psychology, though he never did portraits on commission, preferring to choose his sitters from among his friends and relatives.

This portrait shows Degas's lifelong friend Henri Rouart, whom he had met when they attended the elite lycée Louis le Grand in Paris between 1845 and 1853. After graduation they pursued separate careers, Degas taking up the law for a year before beginning to paint, Rouart joining the military and then going into engineering. During the Franco-Prussian war in 1870–71 Degas, who had volunteered for the army, was made a lieutenant under Rouart's command. After the armistice, Degas dined at least once a week at Rouart's house. He painted his friend three times, his wife and family many more. A letter he wrote to Rouart reveals the depths of Degas's friendship: "The heart is like many an instrument," he wrote, "it must be rubbed up and used a lot so that it keeps bright and well. For my own it is rather you who rubs it than its owner."

This portrait reveals Degas's admiration for his friend and his accomplishments. Rouart, dressed in typical upper-class garb, distinguished and serious, stands in a railroad yard that leads to a large factory in the background. The plant is the Louisiana Ice Manufacturing Company, the first ice-making facility in the United States and the largest in the world when it opened in New Orleans in 1868. As joint head of a successful engineering firm in Paris, Rouart had helped to design the company's aqua ammonia absorption system, the critical part of the ice-making process. Degas saw this facility on a visit to his American relatives in New Orleans in 1871–72.

Degas admired Rouart's ingenuity and his involvement with the brand-new field of refrigeration, but he also respected his friend as a great connoisseur with an outstanding collection of Old Master and nineteenth-century paintings and an enthusiastic supporter of the Impressionists. Rouart not only bought many of their works and helped to defray their exhibition expenses, but he was also a painter himself and participated in seven of the eight Impressionist shows.

PT

Still Life with Brioche   1880

oil on canvas, 21 ¾ x 13 ⅞ in. (55.2 x 35.2 cm.)
William R. Scott, Jr., Fund, 84.8

Pierre Auguste Renoir

French, 1841–1919

Renoir, Monet, and other Impressionists regularly worked *en plein air,* a practice that not only served their interest in painting the motifs of nature, but may also have reflected a French enthusiasm for outdoor experience that generated a vogue for gardening from the 1860s onward. Claude Monet is the only painter from this period with whom garden imagery is widely associated, a result of his labors to create, maintain, and depict on canvas his flower and water gardens at Giverny in the 1890s. But nearly all later nineteenth-century painters made images of their own gardens or those of their acquaintances.

Renoir's *The Garden in the Rue Cortot, Montmartre,* like his famous depiction of *Claude Monet in His Garden* (1875, Wadsworth Atheneum), reflects the painter's enthusiasm for *plein air* painting and for flowers in the orderly profusion of a private landscape. The vertical canvas, less common for garden subjects than figural ones, seems nevertheless to have been planned without figures; for the textures in the upper right indicate that the trees, grass, and suggestions of a fence were completed before the figures were begun. After he added the two figures, Renoir painted in the slender, sparsely foliated tree, which leads the eye from the foreground flowers to the rear of the picture space, establishing spatial recession without obscuring the figure it overlaps.

Writers about Renoir have variously identified the two figures shown in conversation as Renoir and Monet or Sisley and Monet. Whatever the identification, one is invited to appreciate the painting not only as a spontaneous glimpse of the overgrown natural beauty of Renoir's garden, but as a depiction (perhaps contrived) of two Impressionist painters in celebration of their similar goals and interests.

There is some disagreement about the date of *The Garden in the Rue Cortot.* It is often dated 1878, but it appears in the catalogue raisonné among paintings of 1876, the year in which Renoir acquired the Montmartre studio to work on the large figure paintings he had just begun. Georges Rivière, a close friend who accompanied Renoir the day he found the Rue Cortot studio, recounted that Renoir brought models for his large figure paintings to the studio and painted from them in the garden there. Garden images, dominated by flowers but containing small figures, appear in Renoir's oeuvre from the early 1870s through 1876. All of those are horizontal canvases that are smaller than this one, and the figures in them are women. The closest comparable work, a vertical depiction of flowers with a man and woman in the background conversing across a fence, was painted in 1876. After that date, Renoir's interests in small figures shifted toward views of paths in the landscape, the realm beyond the garden that is glimpsed in *The Garden in the Rue Cortot.*

KP

96

The Garden in the Rue Cortot, Montmartre 1876

oil on canvas, 59 ¾ x 38 ⅜ in. (151.8 x 97.5 cm.)
Acquired through the generosity of Mrs. Alan M. Scaife, 65.35

Alfred Sisley
French, 1839–1899

As a young man, Alfred Sisley was sent to London to learn business, but during his four years there (1857–1861) he was inspired by the works of Constable, Bonington, and Turner to become a landscape painter himself. In 1862, he traveled to Paris, where he met Monet, Renoir, and Bazille in the teaching studio of Charles Gleyre. When Gleyre's studio closed the following year, the young painters worked together on landscapes, a subject their master had not encouraged. Of all the artists who became known as Impressionists, Sisley and Monet were the only two who sustained a lifelong dedication to landscape subjects.

Scholars of French landscape painting usually describe Sisley as a gifted amateur, who often followed the artistic lead and innovations of his friend Monet. It is true that Sisley's landscapes, compared to Monet's, rarely surprise with daring points of view or startling dissolutions of form. Instead Sisley's motifs—fields, orchards, suburban paths, riverbank villages—please the viewer with their beauty of subject and paint.

Like the works of Monet and Pissarro, Sisley's vast output of landscapes can be grouped by the specific sites the works depict, most of which are locales near Paris, especially towns along the Seine and its tributaries. Between 1880 and 1897 Sisley lived in or near Moret, about forty miles southeast of Paris and just a few miles south of the forest of Fontainebleau, and he made several hundred paintings there. From Moret, on the Loing River, it was only a mile and a half to the river's confluence with the Seine at Saint-Mammès, where he painted many more views of the riverbanks, barges, and old houses. Carnegie Institute's painting shows the tighter brushwork with which Sisley replaced his broad Corot-like facture of the late 1870s, which is a reason for assigning it a date of 1880 or 1881. This and several closely related paintings were composed to contrast the nearer, grassy bank of the artist's worksite with the clustered boats and houses across the water.

Sisley exhibited his landscapes in four Impressionist group exhibitions, and he shared the Impressionists' struggle for public understanding and acceptance. He earned praise in America before he gained recognition in his own country. For example, the dealer Durand-Ruel included Sisley's work in a successful Impressionist exhibition in New York in 1886, and in 1889 he produced a one-man exhibition of twenty-eight paintings by Sisley. Two years later an exhibition of works by Monet, Pissarro, and Sisley was held in Boston. Such opportunities to see Sisley's work inspired a collector to buy this work, which was later exhibited in the 1898 Carnegie International and purchased for the collection at the end of that year. Its acquisition by Carnegie Institute is testimony to the early American appreciation of Impressionist landscape painting and the art of Alfred Sisley.

KP

Saint-Mammès on the Banks of the Loing   c. 1881

oil on canvas, 21 ¼ x 29 in. (54 x 73.7 cm.)
Purchase, 99.7

Exhibited in the 1898 Carnegie International

Pierre-Cécile Puvis de Chavannes

French, 1824–1898

Painters such as Gauguin, Seurat, Denis, and Redon admired and emulated Pierre Puvis de Chavannes, a nineteenth-century master whose reputation languished after 1900. Puvis's influence on these younger and more significant artists has stimulated recent studies of his work.

As a muralist Puvis belongs to the Neo-Classical tradition that the French Academy sustained through most of the nineteenth century. He specialized in generalized, studio-posed figures in imaginary Arcadian settings, tableaux that evoked a nonspecific and tranquil antiquity. Those qualities are found in the work of many nineteenth-century conservative artists, but Puvis's art offered elements that the next generation of artists incorporated into their own work. Some of their adaptations of his style appear in works that are considered milestones in the "modernity" of late nineteenth- and early twentieth-century art. Paul Gauguin, for example, emulated Purvis's isolated figures in still poses and the friezelike placement of figures in a simple landscape in his most ambitious and "philosophical" symbolist paintings, including *Whence Come We? What Are We? Where Are We Going?* (1897, Museum of Fine Arts, Boston).

This painting is a smaller version of one section of Puvis's commissioned decorations for the Palais des Arts in Lyons and was probably painted several years after the Lyons project. He finished the first section of the murals in 1884, a large canvas called *Sacred Wood, Dear to the Arts and the Muses.* After its exhibition in the 1884 Salon, the canvas was mounted on the north wall of the staircase in the Palais des Arts. In Puvis's mind *Sacred Wood* was the generative image for the three other works in the cycle, *A Vision of Antiquity, Christian Inspiration,* and *The Rhône (Force) and the Saône (Grace).* Puvis's idea was that all art is composed between the limits of antiquity (the inspiration for forms) and of Christianity (the well-spring of sentiment). *A Vision of Antiquity* and *Christian Inspiration* were attached to the east and west walls of the Lyons staircase, where they were aligned with the third of these works, in which male and female figures represent the Rhône and Saône rivers, which converge at Lyons.

In 1897 *A Vision of Antiquity* appeared in the Carnegie International exhibition and entered Carnegie Institute's permanent collection. In 1919 René Gimpel wrote in *Diary of an Art Dealer* of his visit to the Institute: "The best picture is a Puvis de Chavannes: glimpse of antiquity, a celestial epic, with gods and goddesses, herdsmen and goats, Eros, the lute, quasi-winged horses, affectionate dalliance, obliteration of the sky, the earth and human beings before the dazzle and blue violence of a sea which is no more than a vast lake."

KP

Place des Lices, St. Tropez   1893

oil on canvas, 25 ¾ x 32 ³⁄₁₆ in. (65.4 x 81.8 cm.)
Acquired through the generosity of the Sarah Mellon Scaife family, 66.24.2

Claude Monet

French, 1840 – 1926

This windblown seascape, vigorously painted and richly textured, is an outstanding example of Monet's early work. He undoubtedly spent a good deal of time on this beach in his youth as he grew up in Saint-Addresse, a residential suburb of Le Havre from where this view was painted. It was completed in 1868, less than ten years after Monet first decided to become an artist. Its subject is traditional, with its strongest precedents in seventeenth-century Dutch painting, but its style is distinctly modern. He must have thought a good deal of the picture because he showed it in the second Impressionist exhibition held in Paris in 1876.

Monet first divided the picture almost exactly in half between the sea and sky, drawing attention to the abstract qualities of the composition. He then applied his paint with forcefulness and subtlety, choosing his colors with a refined eye to capture the effects of the overcast day and the movement of the sea. The many different strokes in the water, for example, suggest its various states—the rippling surface of the bay, the rise and fall of the wave, and the sheet of rivulets on the beach—and the large triangles of the bay and the eddies on the beach are echoed in the similar shapes of the shore. Above this pattern of brushwork and shape is the sky, which is covered with longer, thicker, more opaque strokes. The boldest ones, like those of the sea, are primarily horizontal, but they vary more in their undulations and placement than those below them, making the sky weightier and even more active than the sea. This effect is enhanced by Monet's use of stronger contrasts in the sky, with lead whites juxtaposed with larger areas of blue and purple.

Although nature clearly dominates this view, as it does in so much of Monet's work, humanity is present in the small houses barely visible on the distant peninsula, in the mooring posts on the beach to the left, and in the traditional fishing boat on the water. Monet has very carefully placed the boat near the end of the large flat area of blue-gray clouds, just where the long stroke of white on the horizon begins to dissipate. Moreover, if one constructed an imaginary square whose left side was the left side of the canvas, its right side would run straight through the sail of the boat, locking it into perfect harmony with the sea and the shore. Whether Monet did this with a measuring device or not, it indicates his sensitivity to the arrangement of his picture. Even the location of his signature parallels the horizon, fills the void of the triangle of the shore, and seems to balance the boat.

This kind of awareness, along with the viewer's firm footing on the beach, separates Monet's painting from its earlier nineteenth-century romantic prototype—the view of the storm-tossed boat. Although Monet's carefully observed scene evokes similar feelings about the grandeur of nature, it is a familiar world in which we have a place and where sea and sky are balanced. It is a world as reassuring as Monet's rich array of blues and grays and as enlivening as his exuberant brushwork.

PT

Christ and the Disciples at Emmaus   1896 – 97

oil on canvas, 78 x 110 ½ in. (198.1 x 280.7 cm.)
Gift of Henry Clay Frick, 98.5

Exhibited in the 1898 Carnegie International

Louis Majorelle
French, 1859–1926

In 1900 the Art Nouveau movement was at its peak in France. Louis Majorelle and other French designers responded to an anxious time of economic and social change by seeking new, innovative designs. They turned primarily to nature for inspiration and brought to their work a springlike freshness and vitality. At the same time, they sought strength for their innovations in their own French tradition. Samuel Bing, whose Paris shop, L'Art Nouveau, gave the movement its name, challenged French designers "to pick up the threads of that tradition, with all its grace, elegance, sound logic and purity, and give it new developments, just as if the thread had not been broken for nearly a century."

Majorelle began his artistic career as a painter and in 1877 entered the Ecole des Beaux-Arts in Paris where he studied under Jean-François Millet. In 1879, however, his father's death forced Majorelle to leave his studies and return to his home in Nancy to take over his father's cabinetmaking business. He produced eighteenth-century style furniture, as his father had done, until about 1895, when, probably under the influence of Emile Gallé (1846–1904), he turned to art nouveau.

Fully conversant with French traditional designs—their forms, the quality of their materials, and the exquisiteness of their execution—Majorelle brought these attributes to his new furniture. It is thought that he worked in clay, like a sculptor, and then translated the model into wood or, in the case of decorative mounts, into metal. The resulting forms, achieved by whatever means, have an organic vitality. They are strong but controlled, and their intriguing curves, twists, and turns offer great visual pleasure.

The original leather upholstery, which survives on the chair, is tooled with a representation of a thistle, the symbol of the province of Lorraine, of which Nancy was the capital. Hence, Majorelle's choice of decoration has meaningful historical roots. Moreover, the plant is clearly recognizable; he has not abstracted it to the degree that some of his non-French contemporaries would have done. The swirling profusion that emanates from the thistle, however, creates for it an abstract background that doubtless expresses nature's potentially threatening force. Thus the survival of the original upholstery is critical to the total impression of the chair as Majorelle conceived it. The thistle's spikes and swirls bring a menacing element to an otherwise completely joyful chair.

PMJ

Armchair c. 1900

walnut with original leather upholstery, 48 ¼ x 22 ⅝ x 26 in. (122.6 x 57.5 x 66 cm.)
Decorative Arts Purchase Fund, 84.33.2

Edouard Vuillard

French, 1868–1940

Vuillard and his Nabi colleagues of the 1890s endorsed a consciously decorative approach to art, emphasizing patterns, the arabesque, and overall flatness and deemphasizing spatial perspective. Vuillard achieved brilliant results with these devices in the production of large, mural-scale panels commissioned by wealthy friends for their Parisian homes. He employed the same techniques in smaller, intimate paintings of interior scenes showing a milieu of modest middle-class people and activities. Though Vuillard traveled widely, he painted only in Paris and was fascinated with the familiar rather than the exotic.

Interior with Women is typical of most of Vuillard's work, an interested and sensitive glimpse into a domestic setting where commonplace activities are being conducted in tranquility. The women seem unaware of the artist and, like most of his subjects, are absorbed in thought or some private activity. Vuillard often depicted several figures gathered around tables, conversing over refreshments or listening to someone play the piano. In this painting they are seen from across the room, engrossed in hand work around a table that provides a focus for the composition. The juxtapositions of patterned dresses and furnishings invite a decorative reading of the painting rather than a psychological one, especially since the figures' faces are defined by only four or five daubs of the brush, and the viewer must stand very close to the canvas to see its details.

What is known about Vuillard's circle of friends and the figures in many of his other small interiors supports speculation on the identities of the figures in *Interior with Women*. One of Vuillard's friends and early patrons was Thadée Natanson, art critic for *La Revue Blanche* and a spokesman for the Nabi group. His wife, Misia Godebska, became Vuillard's lifelong friend and favorite model. Thadée Natanson's two brothers were also involved in new art and theater in Paris. Vuillard knew them and their wives and a likely identification of the three women in *Interior* would be the three mesdames Natanson.

KP

Four Figures on a Pedestal   1950

bronze, 20 ¼ x 16 x 6 ⅜ in. (51.4 x 40.6 x 16.2 cm.)
Gift of Mr. and Mrs. Henry J. Heinz II, 55.45

Oskar Kokoschka

British, b. Austria, 1886–1980

Kokoschka, a daring and outspoken Expressionist, painted many portraits that were executed, like the rest of his work, in a brilliant palette with energetic brushwork. The expressive hands in some portraits—sometimes shown in poses of vain grasping or disconcerting agitation—emphasize the sitters' psychic conflicts. Nearly all are without attributes or background.

The *Portrait of Thomas Masaryk* was painted in 1935–36, at the end of Masaryk's term as the first president of Czechoslovakia (1918–35). The visionary composition includes contemporary and historic figures combined with Kokoschka's vivid landscape style and conveys the artist's strong feelings about the principles on which Masaryk brought about the creation of the Czech state.

In this work, Kokoschka's first intentionally allegorical portrait, the figure of Masaryk that dominates the center of the canvas is, unlike many of Kokoschka's sitters, posed calmly, his hands at rest. Beyond and below Masaryk, to the right, is a scene of Prague whose townscape elements symbolize Masaryk's immediate and tangible achievements in the formation of the Czechoslovakian state. Also to Masaryk's right a large but less corporeal second figure huddles toward him, the right hand gesturing guidance or protection. This figure, identified by letters below his chin, represents the Moravian humanist John Amos Comenius (1592–1670), a philosophical mentor for Masaryk who was also one of Kokoschka's heroes.

Between and beyond the heads of Comenius and Masaryk—in the background of their thought, so to speak—Kokoschka depicted the execution of Bohemian religious reformer John Huss (1369–1415). Kokoschka explained, "By a representation of the burning of Huss in the background the days when prejudices become stronger than all reason, when all sense is perverted into nonsense are warningly evoked." Kokoschka intended the painting to serve a didactic function, with the stable and dominant form of Masaryk conveying the humanitarian achievements made tangible in the Czech state.

At around the time of the First World War, Pittsburgh, with its large Slovak population, was a center of nationalist agitation in the movement to create a Czech state. Masaryk, who had persuaded President Woodrow Wilson to approve Czech national unity and independence, came to Pittsburgh in May 1918 to ensure backing for the nascent state, and prominent Czech and Slovak representatives signed a document called the Pittsburgh Agreement in its support.

In 1937, the year Masaryk died, the Third Reich branded Kokoschka a degenerate artist and confiscated his work. Kokoschka fled to London, taking Masaryk's portrait with him.

KP

Portrait of Thomas Garrigue Masaryk   1935 – 36

oil on canvas, 38 ⅜ x 51 ½ in. (97.5 x 130.8 cm.)
Patrons Art Fund, 56.46

Exhibited in the 1936 Carnegie International

Pierre Bonnard

French, 1867–1947

John Russell has remarked, "The bathroom paintings of Bonnard are as important to the art of the twentieth century as the water lilies of Monet." *Nude in Bathtub*, the last and perhaps finest of Bonnard's many treatments of this subject, is surely one of the greatest nudes of the twentieth century. The extraordinary audacity of color that characterizes the artist's mature career is nowhere more evident than in this painting's dazzling mosaic of oranges, yellows, pinks, blues, violets, and greens. Bonnard's daring chromatic adventures are nearly equaled in their startling originality by a pictorial construct in which perspective and volume are denied and forms are piled up to hover weightless over the flat plane of the canvas.

The woman frequently depicted in Bonnard's bathtub paintings is his lifelong companion, Marthe, whom he married in 1925. Marthe's delicate health and obsessive cleanliness prompted her to spend a good deal of time in the modern bath of their house near Cannes. Bonnard metamorphosed this domestic environment, with its decorative colored tiles and furnishings and comfortably curled-up family dachshund, into an exotic setting in which a young woman floats in a pearly tub, her flesh reflecting the opalescent colors of the surroundings. The model is Marthe, but she is transformed by the artist from a woman then in her sixties to the youthful mistress of Bonnard's memories. The result is a conspicuously sensual, emotional, and dreamlike private evocation.

JRL

Portrait of a Boy   1890

oil on canvas, 59 ¾ x 56 in. (151.8 x 142.2 cm.)
Patrons Art Fund, 32.1

Exhibited in the 1897 Carnegie International

John Singer Sargent
American, b. Italy, 1856–1925

Sargent's range of subjects extended well beyond the narrow confines of portraiture. Among his most original, arresting works are the cityscapes and interiors of Venice, where he made long sojourns in the fall and winter of 1880 and the summer of 1882. Venice was especially popular as a subject for artists during these years, for James McNeill Whistler lived there then, and American artists such as John Twachtman and Frank Duveneck passed through on their European grand tours to study the renowned light and picturesque views of the city called La Serenissima.

Venetian Interior, painted around 1882 in Venice or possibly in Paris, is one of the most beautiful pictures of its type by Sargent. In the dark, cool interior of a palazzo, patchworked with light from the outside, six women and a child string beads, promenade in the hall, and quietly rest, contemplate, or observe passers-by from the window. These are more than just elements in a casually observed moment of Venetian life, or a genre representation, for Sargent treated the nearest woman as he would the subject of a portrait: she regards the viewer with a winsome expression of surprise, as if catching a voyeur in the act.

The sober, dusky palette of the scene recalls the paintings of Velázquez, which Sargent had studied at the Prado on a trip to Spain in 1879. The tenebrous atmosphere—enlivened only by remarkable daubs of pink and orange—and the expressive brushwork evoke another important inspiration, the Dutchman Frans Hals. This places *Venetian Interior* consciously in the Old Master tradition, yet Sargent also worked concurrently in the light-struck manner of Impressionism, which was particularly suited to outdoor views of the canals and churches of Venice.

The prints and pastels that Whistler made of Venice also profoundly affected Sargent's vision. Whistler's 1880 series of etchings, in which he suggested atmospheric tonalities by means of sophisticated plate-wiping techniques, provided Sargent with a model for manipulating light and shadow in monochrome; and Whistler's sparkling, opalescent pastels, with their strokes of iridescent blue and green, demonstrated the creation of variety and incident in a picture.

Sargent's construction of space in *Venetian Interior* is solid, even rather experimental, with the open floor in the foreground receding sharply to the balcony door. In his handling of paint, however, it is his mastery of suggestion and evocation that stands out. Sargent's love of pigment finds expression in the loose, confident motions that sculpt form from light. One of the finest, boldest brushstrokes in American nineteenth-century painting must surely be the slash of orangey light that cuts across the gray-green floor from the unseen window at right.

Although many of Sargent's portraits are flamboyant to the point of vulgarity, befitting the glamour of the Gilded Era, the artist could also be astonishingly understated and restrained when his subject so dictated. *Venetian Interior* is devoid of the narrative genre quality of many contemporary renderings of Venice and its inhabitants. The artist eschewed the sentimental and showy in favor of a vivid but low-keyed naturalism, which, Henry James appreciatively noted, "kept the whole thing free from that element of humbug which has ever attended most attempts to reproduce the Italian picturesque."

EAP

Arrangement in Black: Pablo de Sarasate 1884

oil on canvas, 97 $^{13}\!/_{16}$ x 55 $^{3}\!/_{8}$ in. (248.4 x 140.7 cm.)
Purchase, 96.2

Exhibited in the 1896 Carnegie International

Mary Cassatt
American, 1845–1926

Mary Cassatt, the only American invited to exhibit with the French Impressionists, was a native Pittsburgher. A forceful, outspoken individualist, she pursued a career as an artist over her parents' opposition, and after studying at the Pennsylvania Academy of the Fine Arts in Philadelphia she crossed the Atlantic to continue her training in Paris. Edgar Degas first noticed her work at the Salon of 1874 and three years later invited her to exhibit with the Indépendants, later called the Impressionists. This connection, as well as Cassatt's enthusiasm for the bold patterns of Japanese prints, encouraged her to break from academic routines. "I had already recognized who were my true masters," she later recalled. "I admired Manet, Courbet and Degas. I hated conventional art. I began to live."

Besides creating masterful paintings, Cassatt, through her friendships with major American collectors, was effective in placing works by both the Impressionists and the Old Masters in American museums. She was generally opposed to the jury system, but, as she wrote in a letter of 1894, "I did allow my name to be used on the jury of the Carnegie Institute but it was only because Whistler suggested it and it was well understood I was never to serve, and I hoped I might be useful in urging the Institute to buy some really fine Old Masters. In this hope, I was naturally disappointed." To Cassatt's regret the museum concentrated chiefly on rather academic contemporary works.

In 1922, shortly after Carnegie Institute purchased *Young Women Picking Fruit*, Cassatt wrote to Homer Saint-Gaudens, the director of fine arts, "It may interest you to know what Degas said when he saw the picture you have just bought for your museum. . . . He was chary of praises, but spoke of the drawing of the woman's arm picking the fruit and made a familiar gesture indicating the line, and said no woman has a right to draw like that."

According to this letter, the painting was executed in the summer of 1891 at the Château de Bachivillers forty miles north of Paris. Women picking fruit was a rather common subject in Impressionist circles and was treated by Courbet, Degas, Pissarro, Renoir, and Morisot. In content, Cassatt's version most closely resembles that of Berthe Morisot, where the emphasis is on the women's camaraderie and conversation rather than the strenuousness of their labor. Indeed, female companionship in daily activities was a frequent theme in Cassatt's work.

Stylistically, *Young Women Picking Fruit* seems to have been deeply influenced by a mural of this subject by Puvis de Chavannes, which was exhibited in 1890 in Paris. This connection, and the work's large scale and broad handling of paint, suggest that when Cassatt made this painting in 1891 she may already have been pondering her large mural for the Woman's Pavilion of the 1893 World's Columbian Exposition in Chicago. The central portion of this mural, which is now lost, also depicted women picking fruit and employed many compositional elements of this painting.

HA

Young Women Picking Fruit   1891

oil on canvas, 51½ x 35½ in. (130.8 x 90.2 cm.)
Patrons Art Fund, 22.8

Exhibited in the 1899 Carnegie International

Albert Pinkham Ryder

American, 1847–1917

Albert Pinkham Ryder's great visionary paintings of the late nineteenth century relate in spirit to the atmospheric works of Washington Allston, from early in the century, but they are also so abstract in style and intuitive in feeling that they have been described as forerunners of modern art.

Reclusive, spiritual, and impassioned about nature, Ryder exemplified the dark strain of romanticism in American culture. He eventually lost all interest in exhibiting his work, painting only for his own fulfillment, and instead of living in elegant quarters, like William Merritt Chase's Tenth Street studio in New York, Ryder contentedly kept a small, untidy apartment on West 15th Street, where he slept on a fragment of rug on the floor. He once remarked to his disciple, the painter Marsden Hartley, "I would not exchange these two windows for a palace with less a vision than this old garden with its whispering leafage."

Ryder's birthplace was New Bedford, Massachusetts, and since many members of his Cape Cod family naturally went to sea, the ocean played a significant role in the painter's imaginative life from an early age. Poor eyesight ended Ryder's formal education after grammar school, and his early training in art was equally slight; he received some pointers from a local amateur artist before turning to nature as "a teacher who never deceives."

Around 1870 the Ryder family moved to New York, where the painter lived for the rest of his life. Ryder received criticism on his work from portrait painter William Edgar Marshall, whose religious art profoundly affected his pupil. He was eventually admitted to the National Academy of Design and seems to have spent his four seasons drawing from antique casts. During the 1870s, he began to exhibit his work and made the first of four trips to Europe, all of which seem to have left him strangely unaffected. In 1877, he and twenty-one fellow artists split off from the Academy to found the Society of American Artists, but Ryder gradually withdrew from the art activities of New York. It was not until the end of his life that his work attracted more than modest attention, but the popularity it finally did attain led to so many forgeries that today these outnumber the existing genuine works by about five to one.

Ryder specialized in scenes from Wagner's operas and incidents from the Bible, Chaucer, Byron, Poe, and other quintessentially romantic sources. Yet in all of the paintings, nature is the real protagonist, whose organic forms become anthropomorphic, moving to rhythms set in motion by the artist's mind. Ryder labored long over each canvas or panel, painstakingly applying endless layers of pigments and glazes, a poor technique that has caused many of his relatively few existing works to crack and darken, some to the point of unrecognizability.

Marine is one of Ryder's fine and typical sea images. Two small sailing boats move by night across a murky, melancholy sea. The moonlight glows so powerfully from behind the looming clouds that the boats cast shadows across the opaque water. Working with thick paints and glazes on a loaded brush, the artist practically pasted the scene onto the wood, creating massed forms that he left completely unmodeled. Their details were not important to Ryder, who sought to express a universal feeling, not a particular moment. In doing so he designed a pattern of archetypal natural forms floating in an atmosphere of subtle luminosity.

EAP

Marine c. 1890

oil on panel, 12 ⅞ x 10 ³⁄₁₆ in. (32.7 x 25.9 cm.)
Howard N. Eavenson Memorial Fund, for Howard N. Eavenson Americana Collection, 72.35

William M. Harnett
American, b. Ireland, 1848–1892

William Michael Harnett was unknown to historians of American painting until the 1930s, when Edith Halpert of the Downtown Gallery in New York became interested in his work. Although Halpert usually handled the work of modernist painters, she felt that Harnett's trompe l'oeil depictions of hanging objects, with their strong sense of design and uncanny realism, had affinities with both Cubism and Surrealism.

With Halpert's encouragement, in 1947 the art historian Alfred Frankenstein began to investigate Harnett's work. He soon discovered that nearly one-third of the paintings then ascribed to Harnett bore false signatures and had been painted by other artists. Frankenstein's research, published in 1952 in *After the Hunt,* brought to light a whole school of trompe l'oeil specialists surrounding Harnett, including John F. Peto, a previously unknown figure whose reputation has since come to rival that of Harnett himself.

Harnett's origins were humble, and during his lifetime he never received critical acclaim. He was born in Ireland in 1848 but grew up in Philadelphia, where, at about seventeen, he became an engraver. The fine detail that characterizes his paintings no doubt relates to this early training.

Harnett moved on to painting at the age of twenty-seven, after studying only briefly at the Pennsylvania Academy of the Fine Arts and the National Academy of Design. From the beginning he concentrated on still life and soon came to specialize in intensely realistic depictions of humble objects such as books, prints, writing implements, pipes, and beer mugs.

From 1881 to 1884 Harnett lived in Munich, where he was inspired in part to take up hunting subjects by a school of Munich game-piece painters, and he developed the distinctive style of highly illusionistic still life for which he is best known. He spent the year 1885 in Paris, and in 1886 he returned to New York, where he died in 1892 at the age of forty-four. His career as a painter was thus surprisingly brief, spanning less than seventeen years.

Harnett's imagery is notably masculine: beer steins, pipes, and trophies of the hunt are common subjects. Many of his best-known works also evoke a rural ambiance, and a mood of solitude and even loneliness often pervades his paintings.

Trophy of the Hunt, one of Harnett's masterpieces, was painted in Paris in 1885. It focuses on an emblem of death, a rabbit hanging from a string, whose stiffened limbs and soft fur are eloquently evoked. The effect, however, is less brutal than that of some of Harnett's other paintings of similar subjects.

In Carnegie Institute's painting Harnett gave much attention to the weatherbeaten surface of the backdrop, making much of the contrast between the old, brown, rusty rivets and the bright, fresh, new ones. He painted his signature as if it had been carved with a knife into the wood. Although this painting was widely imitated, even the closest derivative works seem cluttered and superficial by comparison. They lack both the magical recreation of surfaces and the dramatic simplicity of composition found in Harnett's painting.

HA

Trophy of the Hunt   1885

oil on canvas, 42 ⁷⁄₁₆ x 21 ¹³⁄₁₆ in. (107.8 x 55.4 cm.)
Purchase, 41.5

George Inness

American, 1825 – 1894

In March 1898 the great collector of American art Thomas B. Clarke arranged to exhibit fifty of his paintings by George Inness and Winslow Homer at the Union League Club in New York. The show became one of the sensations of the season, and in order to capitalize on its success Clarke put up his entire collection at perhaps the most important sale of nineteenth-century American paintings ever held.

The auction, held in February 1899, offered 372 pictures, including thirty-nine by George Inness and many works by Winslow Homer, Albert Pinkham Ryder, and others. Despite such competition, however, the chief works by Inness brought the highest prices, from around five thousand to ten thousand dollars, staggering amounts for American paintings in this period. *The Clouded Sun*, purchased for Carnegie Institute, brought the third highest price of these works. Even granted that Inness's death four years before had pushed up his prices, these sums make it clear that Inness was widely viewed at the end of the nineteenth century as the greatest American painter.

This reputation came to Inness rather late in life, for his mature work was the product of a long period of development and struggle. His early manner was characterized by tightly painted, rather formulaic landscapes that were heavily influenced by the example of Claude Lorrain and seventeenth-century prints. In the 1850s, after visiting Italy and France, Inness developed a much freer style of painting, loosely modeled on the effects of the French Barbizon school. Abandoning literal transcription, he consciously exploited free brushwork to express personal emotion and to endow forms with a spiritual aura.

In the 1860s Inness converted to the religious doctrines of the mystic Emanuel Swedenborg, and by the late 1870s the increasingly spiritual aspect of Inness's work shows this influence. Swedenborg had described corresponding physical and spiritual worlds that share familiar objects and relationships. Inness's late paintings attempt to describe such a spiritual world in paint: objects appear not solid but impalpable; they are not firmly fixed to the ground but seem to float over the surfaces on which they rest. Colors, while not dazzlingly bright, are radiant and lustrous, endowing each object with an ineffable inner glow.

The Clouded Sun powerfully expresses this spiritual dimension to Inness's late style, infusing its thoroughly ordinary subject matter, a ramshackle farm, with religious meaning. A stone wall cuts through the center of the composition, leading the eye into a landscape of almost flat fields broken up by a few elms and clumps of smaller vegetation. In the foreground are three cows, a flock of crows, and a girl walking on a dirt pathway. A pond is in the distance, illuminated by light through an opening in the clouds. The real drama of the painting, however, lies not so much in these figures and objects as in the spiritual dimension of reality that Inness has evoked through his handling of paint. The mistily painted objects seem enveloped in a kind of spiritual haze, and the scattered highlights that enliven them create an almost magical radiance.

HA

The Tenth Street Studio c. 1889–1905

oil on canvas, 46 ⅞ x 66 in. (119.1 x 167.6 cm.)
Purchase, 17.22

John White Alexander

American, 1856–1915

In 1905 John White Alexander was commissioned to decorate the main stairway of the newly expanded Carnegie Institute with sixty-nine panels that would cover more than five thousand square feet. It was the largest mural commission ever given to an American artist, for which Alexander was paid $175,000, the largest sum any artist had ever received for a single project.

Like Andrew Carnegie, Alexander had worked his way up from office boy to world-renowned celebrity. During his childhood in Pittsburgh, he taught himself to draw by copying illustrations in magazines, and in 1875, he left for New York determined to become an illustrator for *Harper's Weekly*. At first he could get work only as an office boy, though success as an illustrator came quickly. Alexander, however, soon determined to achieve equal prominence as a painter, and to that end studied painting at the Royal Academy in Munich in the late 1870s. His mature style did not develop until about 1890, when he moved to Paris and established contact with members of the Symbolist movement. Soon Alexander became the foremost American practitioner of Art Nouveau, composing his paintings in a sinuous, flowing, decorative manner, with asymmetrical compositions and delicate pastel colors. After his return to the United States in 1901, Alexander was showered with commissions and honors, including the presidency of the National Academy of Design; but perhaps the most notable was the Carnegie Institute commission.

Alexander's subject for *The Crowning of Labor* echoed the writings of Andrew Carnegie, which described how the higher levels of human culture are built up from the toil of manual laborers, and they became the first American murals to realistically depict the processes of modern industry and to attempt to relate directly to the local community.

On the ground floor of the building Alexander depicted laborers in the mills of Pittsburgh, and on the second floor he continued his representations of men at work, with views of more laborers, smokestacks, blast furnaces, trains, and boats. In addition, he included scenes of steel girders being set into place in a distinctively modern form of building, the skyscraper. Above these emblems of human toil he placed floating groups of allegorical figures symbolizing labor and the higher achievements, such as art and science, made possible by hard work. In a series of twelve more panels leading up to the third floor, Alexander represented over four hundred figures in a tableau described by his wife as "the ceaseless, resistless, onward movement of the people."

When he died, Alexander had not yet completed the final group of panels on the third floor. A sketchbook survives with drawings of several allegorical figures, including Painting, Music, Chemistry, and Astronomy, but because Alexander worked without finished preliminary drawings, it is not possible to reconstruct his exact intentions.

Alexander's murals overlap in date with the Pittsburgh *Survey*, a project sponsored by the Russell Sage Foundation that documented the unhealthy working conditions of the city through essays, statistical studies and interviews, as well as photographs by Lewis Hine and drawings by Joseph Stella. Alexander's intentions, however, were altogether different from those of the artists of the *Survey*: rather than seeking to bring about social reform, he sought to make the workers more contented with their lot by presenting in a grand, idealized scheme the ultimate product of their labors.

HA

Victory c. 1912

gilded bronze, 41 ⅞ x 23 x 35 in. (106.4 x 58.4 x 88.9 cm.)
Purchase, 19.5.2

John Sloan

American, 1871–1951

In November 1905, John Beatty, director of fine arts for Carnegie Institute, wrote to inform John Sloan that his painting *Winter* had received honorable mention at the Carnegie International exhibition. Actually, *Winter* had been painted by the now obscure American artist Charles Woodbury. Sloan's entry, which also won honorable mention, bore the title *The Coffee Line*. Although it too was a winter scene it showed not a picturesque snowy landscape, but a wind-blown winter night in Madison Square, where a long line of cold, hungry men waited for the free cups of coffee being dispensed to promote one of the Hearst newspapers. The subject, filled with social reverberations, marked a surprising break from the genteel, innocuous images usually favored for awards at the International.

The jury in 1905, however, contained two advocates of strong, unsentimental painting, Thomas Eakins, the famed American realist, and Robert Henri, leader of The Eight. They awarded honorable mention not only to Sloan for *The Coffee Line*, but also to William Glackens for *At Mouquin's*, a fresh, informal vignette of the gregarious financier James Moore with one of his mistresses at Mouquin's French restaurant in Greenwich Village.

As often proved the case in the early years of Carnegie Institute, the jury of the International, which was composed of artists, proved more liberal and advanced than the Institute's staff. Consequently, the museum that year acquired an unthreatening canvas by the Parisian Lucien Simon but not the pathbreaking works of Glackens and Sloan. *At Mouquin's* now hangs in The Art Institute of Chicago, but in 1983 the Museum of Art finally acquired *The Coffee Line*, the first painting by Sloan to enter the collection.

Sloan's emergence into artistic maturity was sparked by the loss of his full-time position as a newspaper illustrator for the *Philadelphia Press* and his consequent move to New York late in 1904. *The Coffee Line*, executed in the winter of 1905, was the first major painting he completed in New York. Its composition is remarkably bold. Most of the picture is filled with dark elements: a somber night sky, fitfully illuminated by the lights of distant buildings; the black silhouette of the wagon; and the outlines of the men standing in line. Only the snow in the foreground, which is painted with great technical bravura, moves away from a sober palette of blacks and grays.

In its unsettling depiction of poverty, suffering, and social inequality, *The Coffee Line* relates directly to Sloan's radical political beliefs. Not long after he completed the painting he joined the Socialist Party, and in 1912 he became art editor of *The Masses*. Of all Sloan's paintings, *The Coffee Line* most strongly declares his outrage over social injustice.

HA

Picnic   c. 1914–15

oil on canvas, 77 x 106 ½ in. (195.6 x 270.5 cm.)
Gift of the People of Pittsburgh in honor of the Sarah Scaife Gallery,
through the Women's Committee of the Museum of Art, 72.51

Patrick Henry Bruce

American, 1881–1936

Patrick Henry Bruce was one of the most accomplished American painters of the early twentieth century, although his work remained obscure until the 1970s when research and cultural attention gradually revealed him to be an artist of major importance.

Many facts about Bruce remain elusive, but we know that he was born in 1881 to a distinguished Virginia family whose fortunes had been vastly diminished by the Civil War. His early teachers included William Merritt Chase, Robert Henri, and the neo-classical sculptor Edward Valentine.

During the winter of 1903–04 Bruce moved from New York City to Paris; he returned to the United States only briefly, in 1905 and in 1936. After his arrival in Paris Bruce soon became acquainted with the extensive circle of expatriate Americans there, including the Steins—Gertrude, Leo, Sarah, and Michael—whom he met in 1906. Through them he met Henri Matisse in 1907, and he became an organizer and original member of the Matisse School that was started in early 1908.

By 1906 Bruce had begun to explore Impressionist uses of color, and his subsequent associations with Matisse and with Robert and Sonia Delaunay considerably increased his concern with color. His move toward strongly pigmented flat areas of color during the period 1912–16 marks the beginning of his mature work. Only six paintings survive from this transitional period.

Abstract is one of about twenty-five paintings that have survived from the 1917–36 period, during which the intensity of Bruce's creative energies was directed not only toward the careful and precise composition of shapes and colors, but, indeed, toward the perfect painting. *Abstract,* like Bruce's other works from this period, contains his basic repertory of geometric still-life forms, which read as objects on a tipped-up table but which have been abstracted beyond immediate recognition. One of these objects suggests an ashtray with a cigarette, or a mortar and pestle; another seems to allude to a spherical cheese with a slice missing or to a piece of sectioned fruit.

Representation, however, was not Bruce's objective. His paintings of the 1920s are carefully balanced compositions in which the acknowledged flatness of the canvas in some areas is played off against the illusion of depth in others. This illusion is sometimes the result of traditional perspective and sometimes simply created by overlapping elements. The colors in Bruce's paintings, from black to muted tones, exist as themselves, tending to avoid representation, but they are balanced so as to shift the viewer's perception between object and area, flatness and depth. In both the form and color of these paintings, Bruce pays homage to the Italian primitive and Renaissance painters he admired, especially Fra Angelico, Botticelli, and above all Mantegna.

In Bruce's late years, he was increasingly aloof and testy. He suffered from a series of gastronomic and other disorders, both real and imagined. The death of his dearest friend in 1917, and the final departure of his wife and son for America in 1920, were painful blows. Even more traumatic was the vehement rejection of his increasingly innovative paintings by the critics of the early 1920s. He continued to work in solitude, seldom exhibiting his work and showing it only to a few trusted friends. In 1933 Bruce moved from Paris to Versailles, apparently destroying all the paintings in his possession except about twenty-one canvases. In the summer of 1936 he sailed for New York, where he took his own life in November of that year.

WDJ

Sunrise Synchromy in Violet   1918

oil on canvas, 35 7/8 x 54 1/4 in. (91.1 x 137.8 cm.)
Living Arts Foundation Fund and Patrons Art Fund, 56.16

George Bellows

American, 1882–1925

George Bellows turned down a professional baseball contract to study painting with Robert Henri in New York. Although Henri did not include him in the famous exhibition of The Eight at the Macbeth Galleries, many of Bellows's paintings have come to symbolize the aspirations of the Ashcan School.

Despite Bellows's close association with the rebels of American art, he achieved extraordinary recognition in his lifetime. For example, he was the youngest artist ever elected to the National Academy of Design. He also showed in every Carnegie International exhibition from 1908 until 1925 and won awards in three of them. In 1925, shortly after his death and just before a retrospective of his work at the Metropolitan Museum of Art, Carnegie Institute purchased *Anne in White* from the artist's estate.

Bellows made many of his greatest paintings at the beginning of his career, working spontaneously and wielding his brush with the unselfconscious dexterity of a natural athlete. After the Armory Show of 1913, however, which exposed him to Cubism and other modern movements, he significantly altered his style. His designs grew stiffer and more geometric, his colors more garish. The pseudo-scientific compositional and color theories of Jay Hambridge and Hardesty Marratta led him, respectively, to construct his designs in triangular modules that disrupted the natural rhythms of his brushwork and to adopt a more strident palette that destroyed the marvelous unity of effect and subtlety of tonal gradations characteristic of his earlier work.

Bellows, however, did make one positive discovery near the end of his short life—the work of Thomas Eakins. Although Robert Henri had energetically championed Eakins, Bellows did not see much of his work until the Metropolitan Museum of Art staged the first Eakins retrospective in 1917. This encounter had an immediate and positive impact. Bellows began to ignore his gimmicky formulas for manipulating form and color and to concentrate instead on the simple portrayal of character. His most impressive late works were portraits of his family and a few intimate friends.

Bellows painted *Anne in White,* one of the most straightforward of these portraits, at Woodstock, New York, during the productive summer of 1920, when he had few distractions from painting. Anne, the eldest of the artist's two daughters, was his favorite model at this time in her life, for she posed in at least a half-dozen portraits between 1917 and 1921. She was a gentle, dreamy child, always thoughtful and well-behaved—just as she appears in *Anne in White.* In this portrait she sits in a low rocking chair, wearing a simple white dress, with a Japanese fan in her lap and a black straw hat in her left hand. An open doorway at the right reveals a porch and summer landscape, with sunlight filtering through a vine-covered balustrade whose jarring greens are the painting's sole, unfortunate reminder of Bellows's enthusiasm for the color theories of Hardesty Marratta. Bellows followed his initial conception of the painting, which is revealed in a drawing in the Cleveland Museum of Art, except for some small changes. He lowered the back of the chair, for example, making Anne's pose more upright and alert, and he enlarged the fan in her lap, which acts as a fulcrum for the design.

HA

Anne in White c. 1920

oil on canvas, 53 x 43 in. (134.6 x 109.2 cm.)
Patrons Art Fund, 25.7

John Kane

American, b. Scotland, 1860–1934

"Genius has been discovered!" announced the *Pittsburgh Press* when John Kane's *Scene from the Scottish Highlands* was accepted in the 1927 Carnegie International exhibition. The selection was indeed remarkable, for Kane was a simple laborer who entirely lacked formal artistic training and had never previously exhibited his work. His canvas, chosen from over 400 entries by most of the major painters of the day, was the only work by a Pittsburgh artist to be admitted to the show.

Reporters soon traced the artist to his shabby one-room apartment by the railroad tracks in Pittsburgh's market district, where Kane had painted for years without an audience or recognition. Suddenly, he became a national celebrity. In the next several years he participated in four more Internationals, and in 1928, 1929, and 1932 he won prizes in the Annual Exhibition of the Associated Artists of Pittsburgh. Outside the city he exhibited at Harvard University, The Art Institute of Chicago, the Cincinnati Art Museum, the Whitney Museum of American Art, and The Museum of Modern Art. By 1930 he had sold paintings to such well-heeled clients as Mrs. John D. Rockefeller, Jr., and John Dewey, chairman of the department of philosophy at Columbia University.

Kane himself later remarked, "If I had tried the world over for an exhibition to show my work I couldn't have found a better one than that International, right here in Pittsburgh." He was by no means overwhelmed, however, by the honors that came his way. "I have lived too long the life of the poor," he noted, "to attach undue importance to the honors of the art world or to any honors that come from man and not from God."

Scene from the Scottish Highlands was selected for the International at the insistence of juror Andrew Dasburg, whose own work consisted of cubist landscapes of New Mexico modeled after Picasso and Cézanne. Dasburg won his goal only after threatening to veto all the other selections. To demonstrate good faith, he purchased Kane's painting for his own collection.

Dasburg's enthusiasm for the painting was clearly influenced by his exposure to modern European art, which evolved from a visit to Paris in 1910 and encounters with Matisse and with Leo and Gertrude Stein. He certainly knew of the work of the French primitive Henri Rousseau, who had been championed by Picasso in a precedent for Dasburg's support of Kane's work. Folk art at this time was still intimately linked with the development of modern art, and Kane, the first American folk artist to win fame in his own lifetime, was also the last to exhibit with the most progressive American painters.

Carnegie Institute today houses the largest single collection of Kane's work, including *Scene from the Scottish Highlands,* the painting that brought him his first recognition. Kane, who had spent most of his childhood in Scotland, noted in an oddly spelled letter to Dasburg, that the painting was a recollection of the days when "I run about the boghs and highlands in bonny Scotland when I was a wee Laddie." In the same letter Kane noted that he himself preferred to title the painting "Braw Wee Heilun Lasses." Kane painted several other scenes of kilt-clad Scottish dancers, several of which depict the annual Scottish festival in Pittsburgh's Kennywood Park.

HA

Larimer Avenue Bridge   1932

oil on canvas, 31 $\frac{15}{16}$ x 41 $\frac{7}{8}$ in. (81.1 x 106.4 cm.)
Patrons Art Fund, 54.30

Arthur G. Dove
American, 1880–1946

Arthur Dove is recognized today as one of the great pioneers of abstract art in America. He studied art at Cornell University, and when he graduated in 1903 he moved to New York City where he began a career as a free-lance illustrator. *Harper's, Life,* and *The Saturday Evening Post* clamored for his sketches, but he grew bored with commercial art and departed for France with his bride in the fall of 1907.

During Dove's eighteen-month stay in Paris he encountered every advanced trend in painting and met the group of American modernists whose influence would be decisive in the United States: Patrick Henry Bruce, Max Weber, and especially Alfred Maurer, with whom Dove developed a close relationship. About a year after Dove returned to New York in 1909, Alfred Stieglitz included him in an important show at the Gallery 291 that featured other modernists such as John Marin, Marsden Hartley, and Edward Steichen.

At a time when American taste was hostile to abstraction, Stieglitz supported these artists and encouraged the development of their theories. Dove's ideas recall those expressed by Wassily Kandinsky in his seminal treatise on abstraction, *On the Spiritual in Art.* Dove, for example, believed that objects possessed both an outer reality and an inner, essential "spirit." A work of art thus portrayed the concrete world as well as the artist's inner mental and emotional universe. Dove considered the emotional factor the informing principle: "We certainly seem to set down a self-portrait of our own inner feelings with everything we do." Moreover, the "color condition," or "condition of light," represented an object's essence better than any details of its outer appearance could.

Dove rapidly evolved a personal style, based on these theories. Between 1911 and 1914 he painted a series of "Abstractions," some of which were completely nonfigurative, which place him among the first artists to work in a totally abstract idiom. In the 1920s he experimented with Cubism and in that decade also created remarkable collages and constructions—made from sand, pine cones, shingles, real and artificial flowers, embroidery, shells, felt insoles, corduroy, chicken wire, and so forth—that recall the assemblages of the Dadaists.

Dove's consistent use of the configurations of nature as filters for his visionary sensibility is exemplified in *Tree Forms.* Working in the soft, blurry medium of pastel, the artist compressed the forms across the surface in an overall abstract pattern. The shapes across the bottom evoke leaves, while those at the top suggest the bark and knotholes of a tree trunk. The grays, greens, and browns convey a sense of organic growth and decay more powerfully than could any "realistic" rendering, and the fact that Dove chose to make the image on wood underscores its association with the natural world.

EAP

Tree Forms 1928

pastel on panel, 25 ¼ x 29 ¾ in. (64.1 x 75.6 cm.)
Gift of Mr. and Mrs. James H. Beal, 60.3.2

Georgia O'Keeffe

American, b. 1887

Georgia O'Keeffe has attained almost mythic stature through her powerful paintings, which establish her as the first great female American artist, and through the haunting photographs taken of her by Alfred Stieglitz and others. She is a last survivor of the small band of early modernists in the United States, having outlived by nearly half a century her companions of that period.

Born in Sun Prairie, Wisconsin, in 1887, O'Keeffe was educated in convent and Episcopal schools and then studied painting at The Art Institute of Chicago and at Teacher's College of Columbia University and the Art Students League in New York. Most of her training was academic and conventional until she learned of the ideas of Arthur Wesley Dow in 1912.

Dow, an associate of the Orientalist Ernest Fenollosa, stressed not realism but principles of arrangement. While not a modernist himself, Dow paved the way for an abstract approach to painting. He once wrote, "Art is decadent when designers and painters lack inventive power and merely imitate nature or the creations of others. Then comes realism, conventionality, and the death of art." Deeply influenced by Dow's views and by his compositional exercises, O'Keeffe once summed up her beliefs in a phrase that Dow would certainly have endorsed: "Filling a space in a beautiful way—that is what art means to me."

Under Dow's influence, O'Keeffe began to produce compositions that recreated objects and internal emotional states in a dramatically simplified and abstract manner. In 1916 she sent a group of these works to a friend in New York who showed them to Alfred Stieglitz, the controversial proselytizer for modern art. According to legend, Stieglitz exclaimed when he saw them, "At last a woman on paper!" Not long afterwards, O'Keeffe became intimate with Stieglitz and joined the circle of the leading American modernists of the period.

Gate of Adobe Church was produced in 1929, during O'Keeffe's first visit to New Mexico, whose desert landscape subsequently became the chief subject matter of her art. She was struck by the simplicity and beauty of the Ranchos de Taos Church, which, she once wrote, "is one of the most beautiful buildings left in the United States by the early Spaniards. I had to paint it—the back of it several times, the front once. I often painted fragments of things because it seemed to make my statement as well or better than the whole could. And I long ago came to the conclusion that even if I could put down accurately the thing that I saw and enjoyed, it would not give the observer the kind of feeling it gave me. I had to create an equivalent for what I felt I was looking at—not copy it."

In *Gate of Adobe Church,* which shows the front of the Ranchos de Taos Church, O'Keeffe reduced her palette to ochre and earth colors that unite the building and the land. She restricted her shapes to rectangles and crossed rectangles, whose repeated interplay can be interpreted either as a flat pattern or as a sequence of forms leading into depth. At the center she placed a brown cross that serves as both a religious symbol and an anchor to the composition.

HA

Cape Cod Afternoon   1936

oil on canvas, 34 ³⁄₁₆ x 50 ¹⁄₁₆ in. (86.8 x 127.2 cm.)
Patrons Art Fund, 38.2

Exhibited in the 1937 Carnegie International

Clarence Carter

American, b. 1904

Clarence Carter was born in Portsmouth, Ohio, in 1904 and frequently showed in the Annual Exhibition at the Cleveland Museum of Art while he was still in his teens. He graduated from the Cleveland School of Art in 1927, painted for a summer under Hans Hofmann in Capri, and then spent a year traveling and studying in Europe. On his return to the United States he held several teaching positions in Cleveland until 1938, when he was appointed to the faculty of the College of Fine Arts at Carnegie Institute of Technology (now Carnegie-Mellon University) in Pittsburgh.

Carter received his greatest recognition in the 1930s and early 40s, when he worked in the American regionalist manner enlivened by occasional Surrealist touches, but his success waned in the late 1940s as regionalism became unpopular and interest shifted to radically abstract styles. Consequently, from 1944 to 1959, Carter worked largely on advertising projects. By the early 1960s, when he returned to painting full time, he had shifted to a more strongly abstract and Surrealist manner.

War Bride, which Carter painted in 1940, is one of his strongest works, combining his feeling for the American scene with his interest in Surrealism. Painted just before America entered the war, it was inspired by a tour of a Pittsburgh steel mill. Carter has written of this experience: "The mills were going full blast. . . . That night I dreamed I painted a picture that was very vivid in my mind. . . . Some of the girls in my senior painting classes were getting married before the boys would be leaving to go into the coming war. This got mixed into my dream painting of the steel mill which became the sanctuary. Edward Alden Jewell was in Pittsburgh at that time to give a lecture on the Carnegie International. We were friends and after the lecture we got together and he asked to go up to my studio and see what I was doing. On the way up I told him that I had been invited for the Annual Exhibition of Contemporary Art at the Whitney Museum but did not know what to send. When he saw the *War Bride* which I was then calling *Bride In A Mechanized World* he said send that and call it *War Bride* and it will be a hit, which it was."

As a result of this exhibition the painting was widely discussed in the New York press and was featured on the cover of *Art Digest,* which described it as "the most incongruous picture of the year."

HA

War Bride   1940

oil on canvas, 36 x 54 ⅛ in. (91.4 x 137.5 cm.)
Richard M. Scaife American Painting Fund and Paintings Acquistion Fund, 82.6

Burgoyne Diller
American, 1906–1965

In 1933 Hans Hofmann, the great teacher of several generations of American painters, wrote, "Burgoyne Diller is one of the most promising of the young American painters. His work is based on this clear consciousness which he has attained entirely through his own demand for an expression disciplined to the limitation of the medium. In his work we find not only a strong talent, but the capacity for a consecutive and full development, which is in itself, the source of every tradition." Hofmann thus described with remarkable foresight the economy of means, the strict formalism, and the propensity to work in series that would characterize the career of one of America's best geometric abstractionists.

Diller was the first of several young American artists in the 1930s and 40s to seriously engage the work of Piet Mondrian, the Dutch Neo-Plasticist who was then the world's foremost living abstract painter. Mondrian came to the United States from Europe in 1940 and lived in New York until his death in 1944. Diller met him soon after his arrival, but the two artists were not close. The young American's personal understanding of the Dutchman's art came, rather, from the paintings in the collection of A. E. Gallatin that had been on view during the thirties at the New York University library.

When combined with an American disinclination for theory, Diller's early dedication to Mondrian's work itself—instead of to his spiritualist leanings and utopian ideas about the content and function of art— reinforced his tendency to concentrate on art's formal rather than philosophical issues. Among Mondrian's circle of American followers, Diller has emerged as the one who made the most original and vital use of the Dutch artist's limited but eloquent formal vocabulary of straight lines, right angles, primary colors, and black and white. Diller was not a doctrinaire formalist slavishly following rigid rules, but an artist whose empirical methods produced pictorial inventions that cannot be mistaken by an informed eye as the work of any other practitioner of the Neo-Plastic aesthetic.

Diller's art evolved in three series, each with generic formal characteristics. It was not, however, until the 1950s that he actually assigned names to these series, calling them First, Second, and Third Theme. The Second Theme is described by what Diller called "elements generated by continuous intersecting lines," by which he meant a limited number of rectangles organized within a set of grid lines. The main stylistic precedents for *Untitled No. 21,* in which bold rectangles of red, yellow, and blue are contained within a set of grids formed by the intersection of thin, straight, black lines, are Mondrian's Paris and London paintings of the 1930s. In contrast to Mondrian's sensuous brushwork, an austerity of surface effect in Diller's painting establishes a precedent for American Minimalist art of the 1960s, a movement to which Diller himself made very strong contributions.

JRL

Number 4   1950

oil, enamel, and aluminum paint on canvas, 48 ⅞ x 37 ⅞ in. (124.2 x 96.2 cm.)
Gift of Frank R. S. Kaplan, 54.15

John Graham

American, b. Russia, 1881–1961

John Graham had a double career in which he first championed and then repudiated modern art. Firm facts are not easy to establish, for the artist delighted in fictionalizing the details of his life, but it appears that he was born in Kiev in 1881 as Ivan Gratianovich Dombrovsky. After the Russian Revolution, Dombrovsky escaped to the United States and took up the study of art. By 1925 he had changed his name to John Graham and become a fervent proselytizer for abstract painting. Until the 1940s, Graham was influential not only as a painter but as a writer, advisor to collectors, and mentor to several of the Abstract Expressionists, including Arshile Gorky, Willem de Kooning, and Jackson Pollock.

Around 1942, however, Graham rejected modern art for what he called classicism, renounced Picasso in favor of Raphael and Ingres, and immersed himself in the study of the occult. He also began signing his work Ioannus Magus, often with a host of other titles. Although in his early career "John Graham" had explored modernist styles such as Surrealism and Synthetic Cubism, the work of "Ioannus Magus" took on a distinctly obsessive character, consisting almost entirely of fiendish self-portraits and depictions of wall-eyed women with wounded necks.

Portrait of a Woman, a drawing on tracing paper, is closely related to Graham's painting *Woman in Black,* also in the museum's collection. Graham reworked his designs continually, making large numbers of tracings to perfect and refine every line, and in this case, both drawing and painting show signs of extensive changes and revisions over the course of many years. Significantly, the creation of both works spans the artist's change of identity; each was first signed John Graham and later inscribed Ioannus Magus.

Graham used translucent paper not simply to facilitate tracing, but because he wanted his drawings framed between two sheets of glass and hung so that the light would both reflect off and pass through them. In creations of this type, like *Portrait of a Woman,* he applied delicate touches of color to both sides of the paper. Despite the obvious similarity between the drawing *Portrait of a Woman* and the canvas *Woman in Black,* the work on paper was evidently intended to stand as an independent work.

While working on the drawing, Graham progressively added elements that increased its drama and psychological force. For example, he added shading around the woman's eyes, which increased the intensity of her glance, and he added the wound to her neck, creating undercurrents of violence and erotic tension. Graham was obsessed with wounds, and in the 1950s carried this motif to extremes, depicting women with blunt instruments thrust through bloody gashes in their bodies. In 1961, he noted, "I personally like many wounds on women."

After his repudiation of modernism, Graham worked toward a final result that combines a classical simplicity and purity of means with an underlying mood of ambiguously mixed violence, sexual desire, and anxiety. He himself once remarked: "I may be not so good as Raphael, but there's more tension in my canvases." *Portrait of a Woman* provides a remarkable illustration of the artist's attempt to thus purify and intensify his work.

HA

Cubi XXIV   1964

stainless steel, 114 ¼ x 84 ¼ x 32 in. (290.2 x 214 x 81.3 cm.)
Museum purchase: gift of Howard Heinz Endowment, 67.6

George Segal
American, b. 1924

George Segal's sculpture has most often been discussed with the work of the Pop artists Andy Warhol, Roy Lichtenstein, and James Rosenquist, who came to prominence at the same time Segal did in the late 1960s. Segal's work, however, has little in common with theirs. He usually depicts ordinary people engaged in banal activities, but there is no evidence in his work of irony or satire, nor does he use the commercial techniques of image production that lent the early work of the Pop artists an appearance of unity in style and point of view.

Segal's attitude toward his subjects is almost directly opposite to the Pop artists'. Warhol and Lichtenstein deliberately avoided or opposed the humanist spiritual values that had characterized most art since the Greeks, but Segal's work is resolutely within the empathic tradition of American social realism. Like Edward Hopper, Segal celebrates the heroism and poignance of ordinary people in their everyday lives. The power of Segal's sculptures comes in part from their directness: he uses actual objects—a Coca-Cola machine, a streetlight, a wooden chair—as props for figures that he casts in plaster from live models. The effect is thus strongly realistic, and the almost exact reproduction of his subjects in plaster casts avoids all reference to the ways the human figure has traditionally been portrayed in art.

In *The Tightrope Walker* Segal chose as his subject an athlete in action, but his treatment of her is anticlassical and notably unheroic. Instead of a traditional athletic figure like the *Discus Thrower,* Segal's tightrope walker is a rather dumpy, ordinary woman, whose body shows every imperfection that human flesh is heir to. She is denied not only the idealizing veil of most Western art, but even the glittery, distracting ambiance of the circus. Segal has provided a real rope, and the sculpture is installed realistically above the viewer's head; but there is no roll of drums to accompany her walk, no gaudy spotlights to dramatize her feat, and no spangles on her costume. The ordinary light in which the work is seen is almost cruel, exposing the crudeness of the plaster casting process that has left the woman's face imperfect. The imperfections of the casting process also render the outline of the woman's figure slightly ragged, making it look as if she were wrapped in bandages, like a mummy. Her body has none of the tension and grace of an athlete but rather preserves the slackness of the model as she waits for the plaster to harden. *The Tightrope Walker,* like all Segal's work, exists in an unmistakably real, non-art context with which the viewer readily identifies, but it bears at the same time overtones of death.

JC

Untitled 1977

ink and graphite on gesso on canvas, 72 x 72 in. (182.9 x 182.9 cm.)
Edith H. Fisher Fund, 81.67.1

David Hockney

English, b. 1937

David Hockney is perhaps the best portrait painter among contemporary artists, and his work, as one might expect, differs in several important respects from the traditional craft of portraiture. For one thing he almost never accepts commissions, and for another he paints only his friends. The pictures are thus made, whether for himself or for possible sale, primarily as works of art independent of their subjects; and his attitude toward his sitters is very different indeed from that of traditional portraitists. The paintings are notably informal, often witty, and occasionally even satirical; and it is quite obvious in some cases that the artist is erotically engaged with the sitter.

Although Hockney always produces a recognizable likeness, that is not his primary purpose. Rather he explores the formal problems of picture making, or he attempts to get down on canvas or paper some particularly memorable characteristic of his subject. Because he generally paints only his friends and only for his own purposes, Hockney can be quite unsparing in his analysis of the subjects before him, and he often conveys in his portraits a knowledge of the inner life of his subjects as well as their outward appearance.

In *Divine,* Hockney has almost completely ignored his sitter's public persona in favor of an entirely informal depiction. Divine is a transvestite entertainer who appears in public as a very fat but tightly corseted and enormously buxom woman. In this guise Divine is literally overwhelming, not the glamorous star or the tragic singer that most transvestites prefer to play, but a threatening, even castrating female figure. The voice, however, is tiny, high, and fearful, in outrageous contrast to the actor's appearance. Hockney's Divine is another person altogether, large, immobile, pensive, rather sad—and clearly a man. The only traces of his highly theatrical side to be found are one exaggerated eyebrow and a slightly overblown mouth.

Yet Hockney by no means suppressed the exaggerated theatricality of his subject; he simply transferred it from the person to the painting, expressing it in the brilliant red and blue stripes of Divine's robe and the strikingly patterned wallpaper behind him. It was a masterful choice because against the Matissean riot of color, the sitter's age, vulnerability, and powerlessness come through with enormous force and clarity.

JC